Handwriting Without Tears®
3rd Grade
Cursive Teacher's Guide

Guide to Multisensory Lessons and Activities for...

Handwriting Without Tears®

Name:

Cursive Handwriting

bunny   tow truck   zebra   key

by Jan Z. Olsen, OTR and Emily F. Knapton, OTR/L

Handwriting Without Tears®

Jan Z. Olsen, OTR

8001 MacArthur Blvd
Cabin John, MD 20818
301.263.2700
www.hwtears.com

Authors: Jan Z. Olsen, OTR and Emily F. Knapton, OTR/L
Illustrator: Jan Z. Olsen, OTR
HWT Graphic Designers: Ingrid Shwaiko, Leah Connor, and Julie Koborg

The Handwriting Without Tears® program and teachers' guides are intuitive and packed with resources and information. Nevertheless, we are constantly developing new ideas and content that make handwriting easier to teach and to learn.

To make this information available to you, we created a password protected section of our website exclusively for users of this teacher's guide. Here you'll find new tips, in-depth information about topics described in this guide, extra practice sheets, other instructional resources, and material you can share with students, parents, and other educators.

Just go to **www.hwtears.com/click** and enter your passcode, **TGCH8**.

Enjoy the internet resources, and send us any input that you think would be helpful to others: janolsen@hwtears.com.

WELCOME

The Handwriting Without Tears® program continues to evolve. This *3rd Grade Cursive Teacher's Guide* is the culmination of successes from previous editions, plus many new ideas from our collaborations with teachers, occupational therapists, and administrators across the country.

We appreciate all the educators who bring such drive and curiosity to making handwriting easier for children. Your feedback and ideas have helped shape this guide.

Good handwriting is one of the foundation skills of language development. It is also a skill that regularly goes on public display and one of the first observable measures of school success. With your guidance, handwriting will be an easy victory for children, enabling them to do better in school.

You can help children develop their handwriting skills so they can focus on content rather than on the mechanics of letter and number formation. As children gain handwriting mastery, their writing becomes more fluid and automatic so they can write with speed and ease in all of their classes.

If you are in a hurry, jump straight to the lesson plans for *Cursive Handwriting*, starting on page 50 of this guide. When you have time, there is a wealth of information in the earlier sections that will give you new tools and insights into the handwriting process. As you get further along and see this icon for A Click Away, be sure to visit **www.hwtears.com/click** for more program information and resources.

Please keep the suggestions coming. Your comments, criticisms, and compliments help us learn what we can do to make the Handwriting Without Tears® program work even better for students and educators.

Thanks,

Jan Z. Olsen   *Emily F. Knapton*

Jan Z. Olsen, OTR   Emily F. Knapton, OTR/L

INTRODUCTION

3rd Grade Cursive Teacher's Guide is the guide to the student workbook, *Cursive Handwriting*. The tips and lesson plans here will help you be a great handwriting teacher. In addition to teaching posture, paper, and pencil skills, you will also teach:

- Letter skills
- Word skills
- Sentence skills

With each step, your students will easily learn what is needed to excel not only in the skill of handwriting, but also in the ability to assess their own handwriting skills. Our goal is to help students learn proper handwriting habits and then apply those habits naturally and automatically to all writing experiences.

Pay particular attention to the stages of learning:

1. Imitation (writing after a live demonstration)
2. Copying (writing from a model)
3. Independent Writing (writing without any assistance or models)

You will be amazed by what your students will learn when these skill levels are combined in well-coordinated instruction.

Aa 58 Bb 84 Cc 57 Dd 59 Ee 65 Ff 67 Gg 60 Hh 62 Ii 72 Jj 73 Kk 76 Ll 66 Mm 90

GETTING STARTED
Prepare
About Third Grade Writers 4
Prep Your Space 4
The Handwriting Process
The Intent to Prevent 6
Cursive Skills for Speed and Legibility 7
Developmental Teaching Order 8
Emerging Cursive 9
Getting It Together 10
Scope and Sequence of Cursive 12
Stages of Learning 14
A Quick Look at HWT's Printing Program 16
The Cursive Transition
An Easy Transition 18
A Fresh Start 19
Reading Cursive 20

HANDWRITING INSTRUCTION
Choose Your Approach
Steady Instruction 22
Flexible Instruction 22

Multisensory Lessons 23-33

Wet–Dry–Try...24

Imaginary Writing...26

Connection Inspection...28

Voices...29

Mystery Letters...30

Letter Stories...32

Nn Oo Pp Qq Rn Ss Tt Uu Vv Ww Xx Yy Zz
91   82   64   96   77   78   63   70   85   83   95   71   97

Posture, Paper, and Pencil Skills
Preparing for Paper and Pencil 34
Good Posture Can Be Fun 35
Place the Paper 36
Grasping Grip 37
Looking Out for Lefties 40

Why Children (and Teachers) Succeed with HWT
HWT Cursive Letter Style 42
Unique Workbook Features 44

Cursive Handwriting
What's in the Workbook 50
What You Will Teach and How They Will Check. 52
Cursive Warm-Ups 54

Lowercase Lessons

c and cc 57
a d g 58
h t p 62
e l f 65
u y i j 70
k r s 76
o w b v 81
m n 90
x q z 95

Capital Lessons

C A O U 101
V W X Y Z 102
P B R N M H 103
K J I L G D 104
L D S E Z 105
Activity Pages 106

HANDWRITING ADVICE
Fluency and Personalization 113
Identifying Handwriting Difficulties 114
Remediating Handwriting Difficulties 115

EXTRAS
Report Card Insert 121
Educating Others 121
Teaching Guidelines 122
FAQs 124
Lowercase Letter Frequency Chart 125
Letter and Number Formation Chart 126

HANDWRITING WITHOUT TEARS

Eager to start?
Lessons start here.

Handwriting Without Tears®
Name:

Cursive Handwriting

bunny   tow truck   zebra   key

Need a schedule?
Guidelines are here.

GETTING STARTED
Prepare
ABOUT THIRD GRADE WRITERS

Your third grade students have been printing for several years and are now eager to learn cursive. You can make the transition from print to cursive fun and easy. With the steadily increasing demands of academics, cursive is now more helpful than ever. Cursive can help children write faster, allowing them to get their ideas across quickly and perform better academically.

Developmentally, third grade is the perfect time to introduce cursive because that's when eye-hand coordination is fully developed. It's okay to teach cursive sooner as long as you monitor students' progress and pace instruction accordingly. The best thing about cursive is that it can be used to overcome printing troubles and help students get a fresh start in writing.

When introducing cursive, we recommend you follow the cursive teaching order and start with letters that are familiar from printing. Begin with lowercase letters and teach letters in groups.

Cursive connections can be tricky—but not ours! We've identified just four types of connections, and our program introduces them in a child-friendly manner that children grasp easily. With the help of the Magic C Bunny, our non-slanted simple style and our one-of-a-kind Review and Mastery, children will quickly gain speed, fluency, and confidence.

PREP YOUR SPACE...

By third grade, many classrooms have returned to the standard classroom set-up with desks in rows. Look at your third grade classroom. If you have one of those modern classrooms with cafe style seating, move those chairs and desks for handwriting lessons. Children need to face you to see the demonstration at the board or easel. Ears are shaped to catch sound from the direction they face. This is so simple and amazing. Look at your class. If students are looking at you, they will see, hear, and pay closer attention.

Can all your students see you?

For Third Grade Children

Unlike other cursive curricula, our program is loaded with multisensory learning experiences. Your students will need room to move. Children will participate in myriad activities—including Imaginary Writing, Tow Truck letter demonstrations—and will work together in teams in hope of passing our Connection Inspection.

For Demonstrations

Double Line Chart Tablet
Demonstrate on this flip chart with double lines. Children can practice on it too.

For Multisensory Lessons

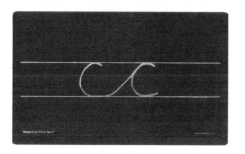

Blackboard with Double Lines
Do lowercase Wet–Dry–Try using these boards. Children can also practice spelling words and play Mystery Letter games.

For the Students

Cursive Handwriting Workbook
Follow the lessons in the workbook. It's loaded with capital, lowercase, and number practice. Your students will love the fun activities that develop their word, sentence, and paragraph skills.

Cursive Wall Cards
Display the alphabet above the board to help children remember letters.

Magic C Bunny
Make the puppet your teaching assistant. Your students can use him too.

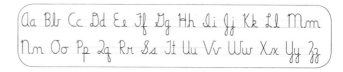

Cursive Alphabet Desk Strip
Place these stickers on children's desks. They help with visual recall of letters.

The Handwriting Process
THE INTENT TO PREVENT

Good handwriting skills result from your thoughtful attention and instruction. Students require deliberate instruction to develop good habits and overcome bad ones.

With this guide and HWT materials, you will be prepared to help students make writing a natural and automatic skill. You'll find that their handwriting abilities and habits vary. Regardless of where they start, you can help students develop and improve their skills:

Teach	**Fix**
How to hold the pencil correctly	Awkward pencil grips

How to form letters correctly	Unusual idiosyncratic formation

How to connect letters correctly	Connection problems

CURSIVE SKILLS FOR SPEED AND LEGIBILITY

You want children to write with speed and neatness while thinking about the content of their work. Would you like to know the secret of developing speed and legibility? Some people think it's about practice, practice, practice, but practicing letters over and over actually makes them progressively messier.

The secret to achieving speed and legibility is following the simple strategies in the HWT workbooks and guides and using the multisensory products. The HWT program develops eight key skills:

Memory — Name letters and numbers quickly from a random list.
Visualize a letter or number quickly without seeing it.

Connections — Connect one letter to another.

Placement — Follow lines and place letters and numbers correctly on the baseline.

Size — Write an appropriate size for third grade.
Make letters a consistent size.

Start — Letter starts in the correct place (either midline or baseline).

Sequence — Make the letter parts in the correct order and direction.
Make the letter parts the same correct way every time.

Control — Writing the letter parts neatly—no gaps, overlaps, or extra tracings.
Keep curved parts curved, straight parts straight, pointed parts pointed, etc.

Spacing — Leave space between words in sentences.

It is clear that each of these skills is important. Children who immediately know their letters or numbers and how to connect them (Memory and Connection) don't have to stop and think. They can write quickly. Children who make their letters sit correctly on the baseline and make them a consistent size (Placement and Size) produce neat papers. Children who always start in the right place and make the strokes the same way every time (Start and Sequence) are able to write quickly and neatly without thinking. (Control) will come naturally as children master the above skills. (Spacing) develops from good instruction and from using the worksheets and workbooks that provide enough room to write.

Speed and Neatness

Music teachers know about speed. It's the last thing they teach. First come the notes, rhythm, fingering or bowing, and finally, practice to reach an automatic, natural level. Then pick up the tempo! It's the same with handwriting. Take a lesson from a music teacher! Work on everything else and speed will come. Children who use poor habits will to be slow or sloppy. Children with good habits can be both fast and neat. That's where we are heading.

DEVELOPMENTAL TEACHING ORDER

Look at the teaching order. It's planned to help children learn cursive skills in the easiest, most efficient way. It's also developmentally planned to start with letters that are familiar from printing. Children learn their lowercase letters first. The teaching order is based on the following:

1. Familiarity of the letter: We begin with seven letters children know from printing.
2. Mastery of the **c** stroke: **c** to **c** is a very important connection in cursive. Learning this connection and letters that use it gets students off to a good start.
3. Difficulty of connections: four letters (**o w b v**) have a high ending stroke and often are difficult to connect to other letters. These letters are taught after the student has mastered easier connections.
4. Formation patterns: letters that use similar strokes are grouped together.

Lowercase
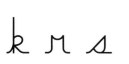

Connecting **c** to **c** is the foundation skill for cursive connections. It is tricky. Teach students to travel away from the first **c** and then slide up and over to begin the second **c**. This skill is needed to connect not just **c**, but **a**, **d**, **g**, and later **o** and **q**.

The first group of letters is familiar from printing and these letters use the basic **c** to **c** connection. Children can easily identify these letters. In both print and cursive, these letters start on the mid line with the Magic c stroke.

These letters are also familiar from printing. The **h** and **p** have been de-looped for simplicity. Letters **h**, **t**, and **p** end on the baseline. They are easy to connect to letters that start on the baseline.

This group doesn't look like the printed letters. Letter **e** is the most frequently used letter. All three use similar stroke patterns and strategies. We keep the loops on **e**, **l**, and **f** because making a loop helps the pencil move in the right direction to connect to the next letter.

Most children recognize these letters from printing. They are fairly easy to learn. The letters **u** and **y** begin with similar strokes, and letters **i** and **j** begin with similar strokes.

These three letters are not familiar from printing. They can be challenging, but if taught using the step-by-step directions, they will not present any difficulty. The letter **k** has been de-looped to keep it clear and simple.

This group has a special name—the Tow Truck letters. These four letters are the only lowercase cursive letters that do not end on the baseline. The ending sticks out like a tow and they never bend down to pick up another letter.

The number of bumps in these letters is important and tricky. When a Tow Truck letter comes before **m** or **n**, use the printed style of these letters. Children should know the difference between the printed and cursive letters.

These letters are used infrequently and can be challenging, so we wait until the end to introduce them. Although **q** uses a Magic c stroke, it is taught here to avoid confusion with **g**.

Capitals

Capitals are taught at the end of the book because of their infrequent use and complex formations. Children usually learn capitals very quickly. The letter style, teaching order, and workbook design make cursive capitals easy to learn.

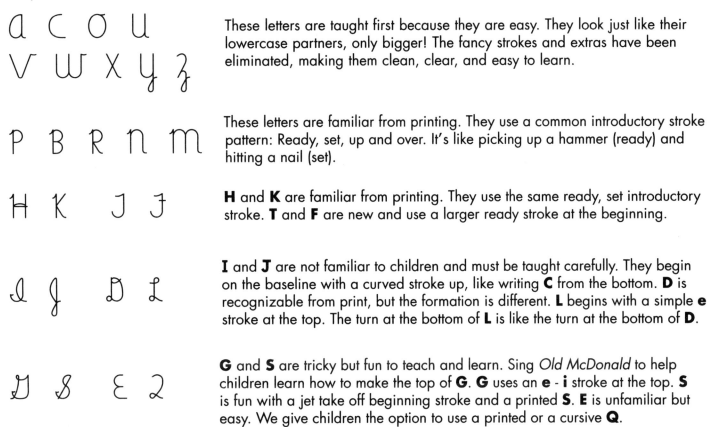

These letters are taught first because they are easy. They look just like their lowercase partners, only bigger! The fancy strokes and extras have been eliminated, making them clean, clear, and easy to learn.

These letters are familiar from printing. They use a common introductory stroke pattern: Ready, set, up and over. It's like picking up a hammer (ready) and hitting a nail (set).

H and **K** are familiar from printing. They use the same ready, set introductory stroke. **T** and **F** are new and use a larger ready stroke at the beginning.

I and **J** are not familiar to children and must be taught carefully. They begin on the baseline with a curved stroke up, like writing **C** from the bottom. **D** is recognizable from print, but the formation is different. **L** begins with a simple **e** stroke at the top. The turn at the bottom of **L** is like the turn at the bottom of **D**.

G and **S** are tricky but fun to teach and learn. Sing *Old McDonald* to help children learn how to make the top of **G**. **G** uses an **e - i** stroke at the top. **S** is fun with a jet take off beginning stroke and a printed **S**. **E** is unfamiliar but easy. We give children the option to use a printed or a cursive **Q**.

EMERGING CURSIVE

In an effort to support emerging writers, we include a model of the cursive capital on the lowercase teaching page to encourage capital letter recognition. Children do not have to write the capital. After children have learned their lowercase letters and connections, they will have plenty of time to learn their capitals.

People often ask us when it is appropriate for children to start using cursive. Typically, third graders are ready to use cursive around mid school year, just before January. Children do not have to wait until they master capitals to start cursive—they can substitute with printed capitals. See the sample below. Notice how the capitals in the sample are printed.

> Over break we went to Colorado.
> It was alot of fun. We had a
> flat tire on our way home. My
> dad knew how to fix it though.

GETTING IT TOGETHER

Most children have no difficulty learning the formation of cursive letters. It is the connections that make cursive a challenge because they change based on the starting and ending places of letters. Other programs also make connections more complicated than they need to be. The chart below shows examples of connecting letters. We believe there are four basic connections that exist in cursive:

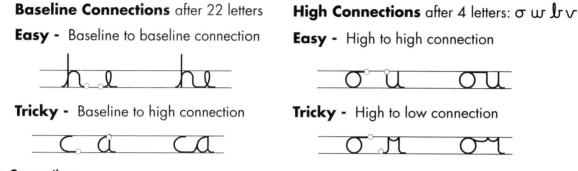

Baseline Connections after 22 letters

Easy - Baseline to baseline connection

Tricky - Baseline to high connection

High Connections after 4 letters: σ ω ℓ v

Easy - High to high connection

Tricky - High to low connection

Baseline Connections

Some cursive connections are easy and natural. You've probably noticed how children write words like **he**, **at**, and **it** in cursive without any problems. As you can see with **he**, it's easy because the first letter, **h**, ends on the bottom line and the second letter, **e**, starts naturally on the baseline. Children rarely struggle with this connection.

The cursive student workbooks begin with a very important connection that requires careful teaching. This is the **c** to **c** connection. It's tricky because **c** ends on the base but then has to connect from the bottom up to the high starting place of the following **c**, as illustrated in the **c** to **a** connection. This stroke is used for connecting any letter that ends on the bottom line to our Magic c group of letters: **c a d g o** or **q**. When teaching **c** to **c** connections, watch out for Magic c trouble. It will look like this:

High Connections - Tow Truck Connections

There are four letters that create the most challenge. They are **o w b** and **v**. We call them the Tow Truck letters, page 81. These letters all end high. Every letter that follows **o w b** and **v** must start high. Letters like **u** that start high naturally, connect relatively easily. But for letters like **r** that start naturally at the bottom, the connection and formation will change. When teaching these high connections, watch out for Tow Truck trouble, it will look like this:

Remember Who's Boss

When teaching connections, it is best to use just two letters and explain how to connect them. Write the letters separately and then write them connected. Explain that the ending of the first letter (baseline or high) can never, ever change. Because the ending part of a cursive letter can't change, we like to say that the ending of the first letter is the boss of the connection. The second letter has to start where the first letter ended, even if that is not the spot where the second letter usually starts.

> I'm the boss!
> Start low **e**!

> I'm the boss!
> Start high **e**!

Does It Make Sense? Try This...

Write the connection, circle whether it was easy or tricky.

o r _____ easy tricky   a r _____ easy tricky   i s _____ easy tricky

o s _____ easy tricky   b i _____ easy tricky   s i _____ easy tricky

o g _____ easy tricky   n g _____ easy tricky   t h _____ easy tricky

w h _____ easy tricky   v e _____ easy tricky   r e _____ easy tricky

Answers:

or - tricky, *ar* - easy, *is* - easy, *os* - tricky, *bi* - tricky, *si* - easy, *og* - easy, *ng* - tricky, *th* - easy, *wh* - tricky, *ve* - tricky, , *re* - easy

Too Many Connections

Other handwriting methods make connections harder than they need to be. In example 1, notice how the method has identified nine connections. These connections also share similar, complicated names: they are confusing for children to remember. Example 2 identifies six connections. Notice how neither method pulls out the four letters that end high: **o w b v**. This causes trouble for children because they never get fluent with the challenging connections.

Example 1	Example 2
Undercurve-to-undercurve joining: *s t*	Swing up-to-overhill: *k n*
Undercurve-to-overcurve joining: *k n*	Swing up-to-uphill: *d e*
Overcurve-to-downcurve joining: *g o*	Sidestroke-to-overhill: *o a*
Overcurve-to-overcurve joining: *y m*	Sidestroke-to-uphill: *b l*
Undercurve-to-downcurve joining: *d o*	Through bottom line-to-overhill: *y o*
Overcurve-to-undercurve joining: *j e*	Through bottom line-to-uphill: *g r*
Checkstroke-to-downcurve joining: *b a*	
Checkstroke-to-overcurve joining: *o n*	
Checkstroke-to-undercurve joining: *o p*	

SCOPE AND SEQUENCE OF CURSIVE

The Scope and Sequence of Cursive defines the content and order of cursive instruction. We typically recommend that printing instruction precede cursive. However, cursive mastery is not dependent on a child's ability to write in print. In fact, cursive is often an alternative for children who never developed solid printing skills. The secret is teaching skills in a way that makes learning natural and fun.

Description

Type of Instruction

Informal/Structured: This is an informal introduction to cursive letters that are similar to print, focusing only on the baseline to baseline connection. Informal instruction also includes teaching children to write their names.

Formal/Structured: Teacher directed activities are presented in a more precise order with specific objectives.

Handwriting Sequence

Lowercase Letters: These are tall, small, and descending symbols. Cursive lowercase letters have more complex strokes, sizes, starts, and positions than print.

Capitals: These are used infrequently, and some have complex formations.

Stages of Learning

Pre-Instruction Readiness: This is readiness gained from printing instruction. A physical approach to writing, along with motor control, should be developed for learning cursive.

Instructional

Stage 1: Imitating the Teacher: Watch someone form a letter first. Then write the letter.
Stage 2: Copying Printed Models: Look at a letter. Then write the letter.
Stage 3: Independent Writing: Write without watching someone or looking at a letter.

Cursive Skills

Primary Skills
  Memory: Remember and write dictated letters and numbers.
  Connections: Connect one letter to another.
  Start: Begin each letter or number correctly.
  Sequence: Make the letter strokes in the correct order.
Secondary Skills
  Placement: Place letters on the baseline.
  Size: Write in a consistent, grade-appropriate size.
  Spacing: Place letters in words close, leaving space between words.
  Control: Focus on neatness and proportion.

Functional Writing

Letters
Words
Sentences
Paragraphs
Integrated Writing in All Subjects

Note about Physical Approach:

The physical approach to writing cursive typically is taught in the earlier grades with printing instruction. In the Scope and Sequence of Cursive, the physical approach is reflected in the Stages of Learning (Pre-Instructional Readiness). If children are still struggling with their physical approach (grip, posture, and paper placement), see Remediating Handwriting Difficulties on page 115 of this guide.

SCOPE AND SEQUENCE OF CURSIVE

	2	3	4	5+
Type of Instruction				
Informal/Structured	X			
Formal/Structured	X *	X	X	X
Handwriting Sequence				
Lowercase Letters	X**	X	X	X
Capitals	X**	X	X	X
Stages of Learning				
Pre-Instructional Readiness				
Preparation from Printing	X	X	X	X
Instructional				
Stage 1: Imitating the Teacher	X	X	X	X
Stage 2: Copying Printed Models	X	X	X	X
Stage 3: Independent Writing	X	X	X	X
Cursive Skills				
Primary Skills				
Memory	X**	X	X	X
Connections	X**	X	X	X
Start	X**	X	X	X
Sequence	X**	X	X	X
Secondary Skills				
Placement	X**	X	X	X
Size	X**	X	X	X
Spacing	X**	X	X	X
Control	*Emerging*	X *Emerging*	X	X
Functional Writing				
Letters	X **	X	X	X
Words	X **	X	X	X
Sentences	X **	X	X	X
Paragraphs	X **	X	X	X
Integrated Writing in All Subjects	X **	X	X	X

* Some schools introduce cursive formally in 2nd grade.
** If instruction is informal, children will not learn skill, for all letters.

STAGES OF LEARNING

Understanding the stages of learning is important to planning your handwriting instruction. Children typically learn in a developmental order. Too often, we find ourselves in such a hurry that we rush ahead. Children learn to write correctly and easily when instructions follow these developmentally based stages. You may need to review some of the pre-instructional readiness concepts below before advancing to the more formal instructional steps that follow:

Pre-Instructional Readiness (Preparation from Printing)

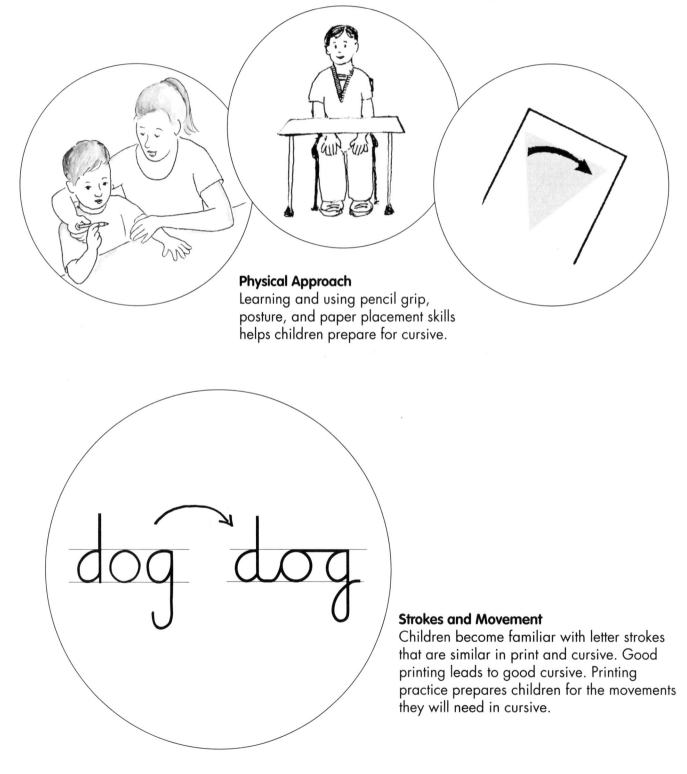

Physical Approach
Learning and using pencil grip, posture, and paper placement skills helps children prepare for cursive.

Strokes and Movement
Children become familiar with letter strokes that are similar in print and cursive. Good printing leads to good cursive. Printing practice prepares children for the movements they will need in cursive.

Instructional Stages

Once the pre-instructional readiness skills have been established, handwriting instruction proceeds in three stages (Imitation, Copying, and Independent Writing). Multisensory activities can enhance learning in every stage.

Stage 1 – Imitation
The child watches as the teacher writes and then imitates the teacher.

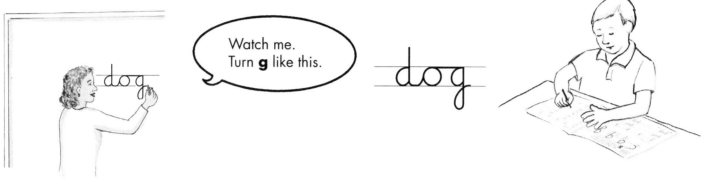

See the motions as the teacher writes step-by-step.

Hear the directions.

See the model.

Write **dog**.

Stage 2 – Copying
The child looks at the completed model of a letter, word, or sentence and copies it, trying to match the model.

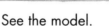

See the model.

Write **dog**.

Stage 3 – Independent Writing
The child writes unassisted, without a demonstration or a model.

Write **dog**.

A Quick Look At HWT's Printing Program

Teachers travel! At some point in time (if you haven't already), you may teach a younger grade. That's why we want to share the information on the next few pages with you. It will show you what our printing program has to offer. It will also show you what children who have used HWT in the past have learned. Keep the information in mind in case you teach another grade next year. If there's no chance of that, perhaps share the information with a colleague or a friend in need of handwriting advice.

We begin with capitals. When children learn to write their capitals, they develop a strong foundation for printing. They learn important handwriting rules (such as the top-to-bottom, left-to-right habit), proper letter formation, and solid visual memory for their capital letters. Lowercase letters are easy to learn because of this foundation.

Children who learn capitals first also learn the following:
- Start letters at the top.
- Use the correct stroke sequence to form letters.
- Orient letters and number correctly—no reversals!

Learning capitals first makes learning lowercase letters a breeze! Think about it: **c o s v w x y z** are the same as capitals; **j k p t** and **u** are also similar to their capital partners. If we teach capitals correctly, we have already prepared children for half of the lowercase alphabet.

A PRE-PENCIL, PRE-PAPER START

Children who have used HWT in preschool and kindergarten have benefited from unique pre-pencil and paper lessons for learning capital letters. There they use the Capital Letter Wood Pieces to learn letter formation. We give these pieces unique names to teach capitals with consistency.

Children make letters with the Capital Letter Cards, Mat, and Slate. All have a smiley face in the top left corner. These tools help students form each letter correctly, systematically, and without reversals.

Big Line

Little Line

Big Curve

Little Curve

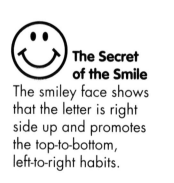

The Secret of the Smile

The smiley face shows that the letter is right side up and promotes the top-to-bottom, left-to-right habits.

RAKE

Capital Letter Card

Mat

Slate

In grades beyond preschool and kindergarten, we teach capital letter language (big line, little line, big curve, little curve) by modeling letters. Say each stroke as you demonstrate the letter. Even children who are unfamiliar with HWT concepts will learn the names quickly.

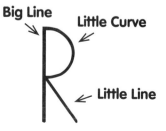

Big Line   **Little Curve**

Little Line

HANDWRITING WITH MUSIC

Music is a big part of our readiness and printing curriculum.
The *Rock, Rap, Tap & Learn* CD is loaded with upbeat songs to make
handwriting fun. The best thing about music is that it promotes movement.
Whether teachers are teaching descending letters or spacing skills, this CD
has all they need to charge up their lessons and catch students' attention.
There is one song on this CD that your third graders will love: *Magic C Rap*.
You might consider borrowing it from a colleague while teaching our first
group of cursive letters.

PHYSICAL PREPARATION

Choosing the appropriate writing tools early can affect what happens to
pencil grip later. We believe in small tools: FLIP Crayons™, Little Chalk Bits,
Little Sponge Cubes, and Pencils for Little Hands. These tools work the finger
tips naturally. Large tools elicit a fisted grip; small tools a more mature grip.
As adults, we write with pencils that are in proportion to our hands. Shouldn't
children do the same? By using these tools and our unique teaching strategies
to develop pencil grip, students can enter your room prepared to learn
cursive correctly.

Teaching Crayon/Pencil Grip

The HWT program makes teaching crayon and pencil grip a priority.
We believe that children who hold their crayons correctly will hold their
pencils correctly. Because this skill is developed at an early age, we
provide teachers with fun songs, fingerplays, and tips for developing
good grip habits from the start. These habits help make learning
handwriting easy.

PRINTING WORKBOOKS

Our printing workbooks are designed to teach letter, word, and
sentence skills. Each workbook has handwriting activities to promote
fluency and the use of each skill. Our printing workbooks also prepare
students for success in cursive. Children who use the HWT printing
program prior to cursive are familiar with letter groups that will be
taught in cursive instruction. In addition, many of our cursive forms are
familiar from print.

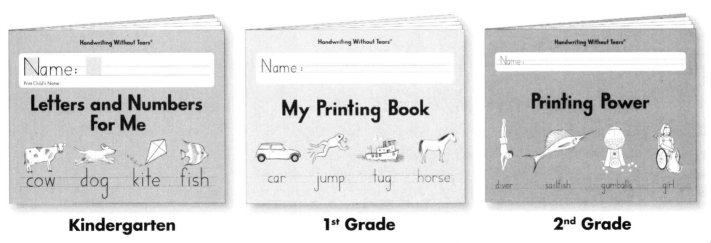

| **Kindergarten** | **1ˢᵗ Grade** | **2ⁿᵈ Grade** |

The Cursive Transition
AN EASY TRANSITION

Using the HWT curriculum, the transition from print to cursive is natural. Children who have learned printing using HWT start cursive with a strong foundation. They have good physical habits for paper, posture, and pencil grip; and an understanding of HWT's unique teaching order that continues into cursive. Even your students who haven't learned HWT will find cursive easy.

Magic C Letters

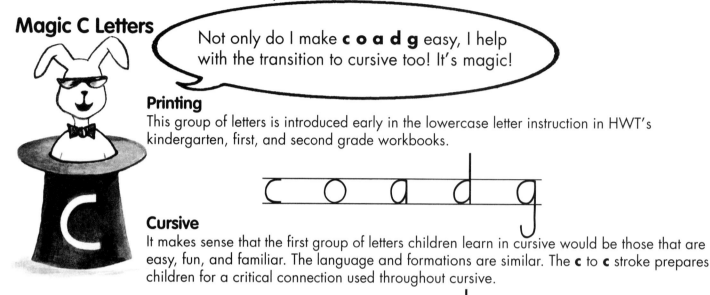

Not only do I make **c o a d g** easy, I help with the transition to cursive too! It's magic!

Printing
This group of letters is introduced early in the lowercase letter instruction in HWT's kindergarten, first, and second grade workbooks.

Cursive
It makes sense that the first group of letters children learn in cursive would be those that are easy, fun, and familiar. The language and formations are similar. The **c** to **c** stroke prepares children for a critical connection used throughout cursive.

Familiarity from Print

In addition, HWT's simple cursive style (no slant, fewer loops, or curlicues) helps children make an easy transition. When the cursive is simplified, many letters look very similar to print. They are also easier to read. Take a look at the difference in letters from print to cursive using the HWT simplified style verses that of other curricula. For more information on slant turn to page 43.

HWT's Letter Transition from Print to Cursive

Another Method's Transition from Print to Cursive

Advantages of HWT's Cursive
Why even teach cursive? Because cursive has many advantages:
1. It's faster because the pencil is always on the paper (except to cross **t**, **x** and dot **i, j**).
2. It helps spacing skills naturally.
3. It has grown-up appeal, so motivation to learn tends to be high.
4. It can help children who never learned proper printing skills.

Whether a child will eventually grow to favor print, cursive, or like both equally is irrelevant. All children deserve to learn cursive. It's a more advanced form of writing that can make their life in junior high, high school, and college easier. Cursive is of particular importance in today's world because we have a generation of children who may not have received direct instruction in print.

A FRESH START
Guidelines for Beginning Cursive Instruction
People often ask us when it's okay to start a child in cursive. Here's what we recommend.

- Formal instruction should begin in third grade, when eye-hand coordination fully develops. It can be successfully taught in second grade if progress is carefully monitored and adjustments are made along the way.

- If cursive instruction begins in second grade, consider waiting until mid-year and teach only the easiest letters and connections (those similar to print, baseline to baseline connections).

- If a child is in serious trouble with printing, consider cursive. Even if the child is only in second grade, it may be better to get a head start on cursive.

- In any situation, cursive instruction should not proceed if the child can't do the pre-cursive activities described on pages 54-55 of this guide.

Using Cursive to Offset Printing Troubles
You may use cursive to overcome printing troubles. In this sample (see example 1), the child is making printing errors (starting letters from the bottom and forming them incorrectly). After the child learns cursive, he is writing with new habits, which has improved speed and legibility (see example 2). We suggest you spend your time teaching cursive to older children with poor printing habits. This allows them a fresh start to use a form of handwriting that is hassle free, and an opportunity to learn something new with proper instruction.

Example 1

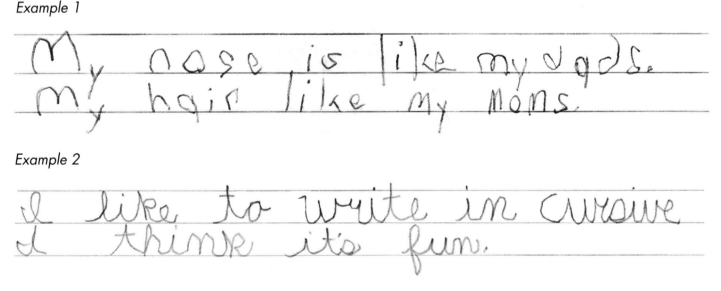

Example 2

Tips
Age: It's best to start in the third grade, but you can begin sooner if you monitor progress and make adjustments.
Coordination: If coordination doesn't appear to be a problem, consider using cursive sooner for children who have always struggled with print. If the problem is significant (even in 2nd grade) make the switch.
Interest: Don't delay the experience. If children are interested in cursive in second grade, give them a taste of it.

READING CURSIVE

The HWT cursive style is very easy to read. We want to help you teach children how to read all cursive writing. Some children naturally make the transition; others may need help.

Teach children that cursive is all about connecting. When writing a word, cursive writers don't lift the pencil off the page, they simply connect all the letters together. But this connected writing requires that some of the letters change shape for an easier connection.

Demonstrate the tips below to help children learn to read cursive. Because many of the letters look like print, they aren't too difficult to figure out. Review some examples and then try some translating from cursive to print.

Super Easy – Here are the cursive letters that look almost identical to print:

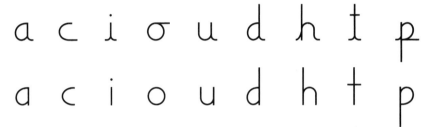

Easy – Here are the cursive letters that look very close to print:

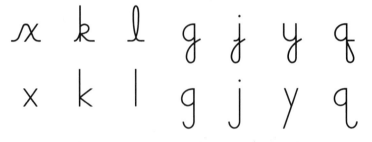

In fact, these letters are so close that you can see the print letter on top of the cursive.

A Little Tricky – Here are some letters that can be a little tricky:

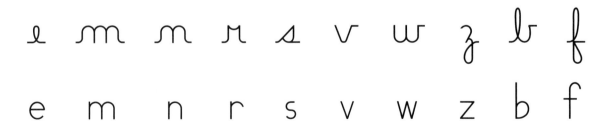

Children will eventually learn to read all of the cursive capitals. But, here are some quick tips:
The most frequently used capitals are at the beginning of sentences or questions: T = 𝒥, I = 𝒥, W = 𝒲.
These are the strangest looking cursive capitals: G = 𝒟, Q = 2, S = 𝒮, Z = 𝓏.

After you have reviewed all 26 lowercase letters with your students, teach them the tricks to **reading cursive:**

Trick 1
Focus on the main part of the letter and not the connection start or ending.

Trick 2
Teach children not to be thrown off by people who have slanted, loopy, or extravagant styles. Tell them to imagine the letters straight or to tilt the paper and then focus on the main part of the letter, not the connection.

Slanted Style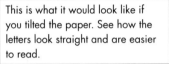

This is what it would look like if you tilted the paper. See how the letters look straight and are easier to read.

Trick 3
Demonstrate how cursive **o** makes many letters look different. Look for letters that follow an **o**. Sometimes they look different. See how the **o** changes the cursive letters listed below. Letters **b**, **v**, and **w** (which you will teach later) have the same effect, but these letter pairs don't happen as often as they do with **o**.

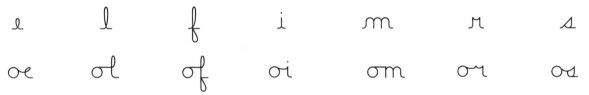

Trick 4
The size of the letter can be a clue. Cursive and print are the same size, except for **f** and **z**.

Small letters are small:

ɑ a, c c, ℓ e, i i, m m, n n, o o, r r, s s, u u, v v, w w, x x

Tall letters are tall:

ℓ b   d d   h h   k k   ℓ l   t t

Descending letters are lower:

g g   j j   p p   q q   y y

The only letters that don't match in size are ℓ = f and ʒ = z.

Try It. Do this exercise with children by having them translate from the board.
Change *cursive* to print:

c a d g j t p e l f u y i j k r s o w b v m n x q z

Now try it with some words: *one   left   more   nose   old   toe   soft*

HANDWRITING INSTRUCTION
Choose Your Approach

The appropriate approach to handwriting instruction is one that is best for you and your students. Teachers, like students, come to third grade handwriting with different skills, interests, styles, and experiences.

New to Handwriting Instruction?
Many teachers were never taught to teach handwriting. In fact, 90 percent of teachers surveyed say they don't feel qualified to teach handwriting. Regardless of your experience, you can be successful this year with a steady, consistent approach.

Veteran Teacher of Handwriting?
Some teachers have strong skills for teaching handwriting and assessing their students' handwriting needs. They have developed an approach that works and can easily adapt to meet individual and class differences. These teachers like to try new things and are good problem solvers. If this describes you, then you should take a flexible, varied approach to handwriting.

STEADY INSTRUCTION

You—new to handwriting, a little unsure
Your students—some with strong skills; others with weak skills and poor habits

How to Do It
1. Read this guide carefully.
   - Use the Posture, Paper, and Pencil Skill activities on pages 34-41.
2. Follow the *Cursive Handwriting* workbook page by page.
   - Follow a pace that suits your class for lowercase, word, sentence, and activity pages.
   - Teach capital letters.
3. Use all the suggested multisensory lessons to support your teaching.

FLEXIBLE INSTRUCTION

You—trained and experienced in handwriting instruction
Your students—some with strong skills; others with weak skills and poor habits

How to Do It
1. Scan this guide, looking for new ideas or information.
   - Use the Posture, Paper, and Pencil Skill activities on pages 34-41.
2. Follow a flexible approach to *Cursive Handwriting*.
   - Teach lowercase letters.
   - Teach the whole book quickly, using only the letter sections and a word or two.
   - Re-teach the whole book slowly from the beginning doing word, sentence, and activity pages.
   - Teach capital letters.
   - Integrate handwriting instruction with reading or other language arts activities.
3. Choose selected multisensory lessons to support your teaching.

Tip:
   - Don't skip pre-cursive exercises...all children need practice holding their pencils correctly. See page 54 for more information.

Multisensory Lessons

Research supports the importance of multisensory teaching to address children's diverse learning styles: visual, tactile, auditory, and kinesthetic. We encourage you to include the multisensory activities in the classroom to appeal to different learning styles and make lessons more fun.

The Handwriting Without Tears® program goes beyond typical multisensory instruction. Our strategies and materials are exceptional and uniquely effective at facilitating dynamic classrooms. Here are just a few teaching methods:

Visual
- Step-by-step illustrations of letter formations give clear visual direction.
- Clean, uncluttered black and white pages are presented in a visually simple format.
- Illustrations in workbooks face left to right, promoting left-to-right directionality.

Tactile
- Wet–Dry–Try on a slate or blackboard gives children touch and repetition without boredom.
- Step-by-step workbook models are big enough for finger tracing.
- The frame of the Slate helps children make lines and keep letters and numbers well proportioned.

Auditory
- Consistent, child-friendly language helps children learn and remember easily.
- Music and different voices promote memorable and entertaining letter instruction.
- Unique Mystery Letters delay the auditory letter cue to prevent children from using bad habits.

Kinesthetic
- Music and movement teach letter formation.
- Door Tracing and Imaginary Writing teach using large arm movements and visual cues.

Goodbye to boring handwriting drills. Hello to fun and achievement! We assigned an interactive activity to each letter lesson. Don't be limited by our suggestions. You can use most of the activities with all letters.

Below is the list of our multisensory lessons that are described on the following pages.
- Wet–Dry–Try
- Imaginary Writing
- Connection Inspection
- Voices
- Mystery Letters
- Letter Stories
- Tow Truck Letters*

*These lessons are specific to a group of letters and are included with the letter lessons for each group.

Tips
- Prepare ahead
- Be dynamic and silly
- Sing
- Encourage your students to participate
- Share techniques with parents
- Create your own activities

WET-DRY-TRY

We emphasize placing letters correctly because it is essential for neat and fast cursive. We teach on double lines because it is the easiest way to impart a sense for how letters should be placed. These Wet–Dry–Try activities on double lines are a great way to teach letter size and place. The image to the right gives you the basics of how we discuss letter size and placement. For additional information, please see page 48 of this guide. Wet–Dry–Try activities appeal to all learning styles and are a fun way to practice letters.

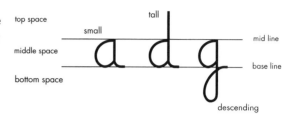

Blackboard with Double Lines

Preparation
1. Prepare Blackboards with the letter you will be teaching.
2. Place Little Chalk Bits and Little Sponge Cubes around the room so children can reach them easily.

Directions

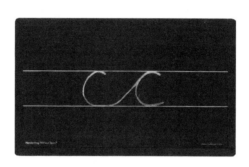

Teacher's Part
Demonstrate correct letter formation.

Student's Part

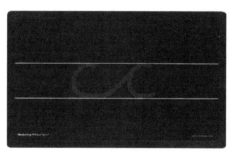

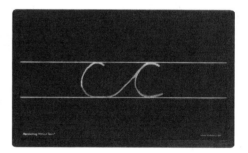

WET	**DRY**	**TRY**
• Wet a Little Sponge Cube. • Squeeze it out. • Trace the letter with the sponge. • Wet your finger and trace again.	• Crumple a little paper towel. • Dry the letter a few times. • Gently blow for final drying.	• Take a Little Chalk Bit. • Use it to write the letter.

Tips
- Use consistent words to describe the strokes. Match your verbal cues to the directions on the letter lesson pages of the workbook.
- Use Little Sponge Cubes and Little Chalk Bits to help children develop proper pencil grip.
- Squeeze the sponge well or the letter will be too wet.
- When using this activity with the whole class, pre-mark students' chalkboards with the lowercase letter (so they have a correct model to wet), and then demonstrate once for everyone.

Other Blackboard Activities

In addition to doing the Wet–Dry–Try activity with a single lowercase letter, you can help children with bumping the lines, placing letters in words, placing capitals on lines, writing names, and more. Below are some easy, fun exercises to get started.

Under Over

Help children stay in the lines with this simple exercise.

1. Do the activity just as you would do Wet–Dry–Try with a letter.
2. Draw an under-to-over curve on the board that starts at the baseline, goes up and travels on the mid line.

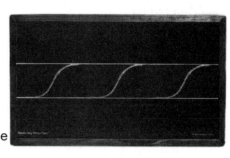

Try straight diagonal lines (for the start of cursive **s**) and Magic C strokes on the double lines, too.

Names and Capitalized Words

Demonstrate/Imitate: Title Case (Two Boards)

1. Demonstrate the child's name on one board as the child imitates on the other.

This activity helps children learn to write their names on double lines before transitioning to paper. Practice writing capital letters and their lowercase partners on the blackboard when you teach the lowercase letter page.

Word Skills

You can help children learn proper letter spacing and letter placement.

1. Point children to the top, middle, and bottom spaces on the board.
2. You can help with word placement by preparing the board with words specific to each space. For example, the word **cows** teaches the middle space. The word **tall** teaches the top space. The word **jog** teaches the bottom space.
3. Challenge your students by thinking of words with letters that occupy all three spaces. The word **dog** is an example.

IMAGINARY WRITING

Imaginary writing is a kinesthetic strategy with visual and auditory components. The picking up and holding of pencils adds a tactile component. This strategy allows you to watch the entire class and ensure that all students are making letters correctly.

Air Writing

Preparation
Learn *Air Writing*, Track 3, from the *Rock, Rap, Tap & Learn* CD.

Directions
1. Sing to prepare the class for participation.
2. Review a letter or number. Trace it in the air in front of your class.
3. Have students hold a pencil correctly in the air. Everyone checks pencil grips.
4. Retrace the letter or number again with your students.

Tip
If you are facing your students, make the letter backward in relation to you so that the letter will be correct from your students' perspective.

My Teacher Writes

Preparation
Gather chalk or markers for a large board or easel. Use *My Teacher Writes*, Track 21, from the *Rock, Rap, Tap & Learn* CD.

Directions
1. Children sing as you stand in front of the class:
   My teacher writes a letter (number) for me
   What's this letter (number) let's look and see
2. Review a letter or number and trace it in the air or on the board.
3. Have students hold a pencil correctly in the air. Everyone checks pencil grips.
4. Retrace the letter or number again with your students.

Tip
If you are facing your students and doing Air Writing, make the letter backward in relation to you so the letter will be correct from your students' perspective.

Follow the Ball

Preparation

Find a brightly colored cup or ball.

Directions

1. Have students hold a pencil correctly in the air. Everyone checks pencil grips.
2. Face the class and hold up a cup or ball.
3. Have students point their pencils at the cup or ball.
4. Write the letter in the air slowly, giving the directions.
5. Have students follow along with their pencils, saying the directions with you.

Tips

- If you are facing your students, make the letter backward in relation to you so that the letter will be correct from your students' perspective.
- Hold the cup or ball in your right hand, out to your right side at eye level. Stand still.
- Say the steps and letters, perhaps: "Magic c, up like a helicopter, up higher, slide down, bump, travel away. This is lowercase **d**."

Laser Letters

Preparation

Gather a laser pointer and chalk or markers for a large board or easel.

Directions

1. Write a large letter on a board or easel, giving step-by-step directions.
2. Have students hold a pencil correctly in the air. Everyone checks pencil grips.
3. Move to the back of room, and point the laser to the start of the letter.
4. Have students point their pencils to the laser dot at the start of the letter.
5. Use the laser to trace the letter slowly, giving step-by-step directions.
6. Have students follow with their pencils, saying the directions along with you.

Note: You may decide to allow students to use the laser with your supervision.

Tips

Laser letters are ideal for teaching tricky letters because they enable children to see the following:

- You writing the large letter first
- The laser pointing to the start of the completed letter
- The laser moving along the completed letter

CONNECTION INSPECTION

Bring cursive connections to life by turning children into words. They will be the letters; their arms the connections. For letters that end on the baseline, keep left hand down low. For letters that end up high (Tow Truck letters - o b v w), put the left arm out. Explain to the next student (letter) that they have to start wherever the previous letter ends. Remember who's the boss of the connection—the first letter (see reminder below). If the hand is down, reach down. Arm up, put arm up. Play this unique activity in teams of four, and allow children to problem solve together in order to pass inspection!

Preparation

1. Choose words to connect/inspect (See word lists on pages 69, 75, 80, 89, 94, 99 of this guide).
2. Write the words on the board.
    - Write them in cursive for an easy start.
    - Write them in print for a challenge.

Directions

1. Divide your class into teams.
2. Choose one student (with the teacher's help) to be the inspector.
3. Write words on the board.
4. Have the teams solve the word problems. Connect them by becoming the letters/connections.
5. Wait for the inspection.

A Reminder of Who's Boss

When teaching connections, it is best to use just two letters and explain how to connect them. Write the letters separately and then write them connected. Explain that the ending of the first letter (low or high) can never, ever change. Because the ending part of a cursive letter can't change, we like to say that the ending of the first letter is the boss of the connection. The second letter has to start where the first letter ended, even if that is not the spot where the second letter usually starts.

Tips

- For more of a challenge, try longer words.
- Choose really long words, print them on the board, and see if your class can connect them.
- Give children time to solve the problem. If it is a printed word, model the cursive form for them.

VOICES

Even with the child-friendly language in the HWT program, the steps for forming letters can get a little boring. Repeating those step-by-step directions using different voices makes it fun and helps solidify the steps in students' minds.

Preparation

1. Pre-mark the double lines on the chalkboard.
2. Begin at the far left of the board.
3. Have students open their workbooks to find the step-by-step directions for forming the letter you have chosen.

Directions

| Magic c
bump the line | up like a | bump! | back down
bump
travel away |

1. Demonstrate the step-by-step letter formation.
2. Say the words that are in the workbook, and ask children to say the words with you.
3. Repeat the activity using the following voices:
   - **high**
   - **low**
   - **loud**
   - **soft**
   - **slow**
   - **fast**

Tips

- Allow your students to pick the voice for the class to use. Make it even more fun by trying voices that are spooky, shaky, robotic, etc.
- Teach with voices using the Magic C Bunny by having the bunny whisper in your ear the voice the children should use.

MYSTERY LETTERS

You can play Mystery Letters with children as a fun way to develop good habits. Mystery Letter lessons are for teaching correct letter formation. The secret is making the first stroke correctly before telling children the name of the letter they're going to make. This ensures that students start the letter correctly and consistently.

Lowercase

Preparation
1. Gather Blackboard with Double Lines, Little Chalk Bits, and tissues for erasing.
2. Use the directions below.
3. Optional: For children who need extra help, you can make the first stroke for them to trace.

Directions

Magic c Letters (See page 61)

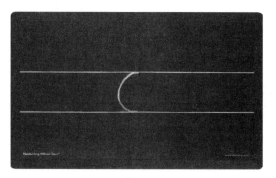

For letters **c a d g o q**
Magic c, wait. Turn it into _____.

Magic c Words

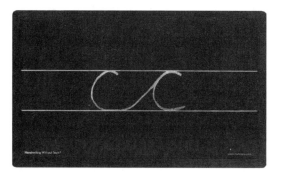

Using **c a d g o q**
Magic c, turn it into _____.
Magic c, turn it into _____.
Add letter _____.

Other Lowercase Letters

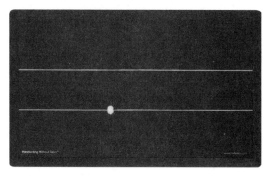

For letters **b e f h i j k l m n p r s t x**
Start down low, travel (up or on the line).
Turn it into _____.

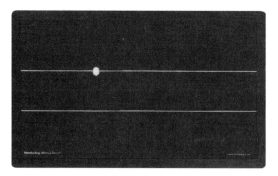

For letters **a c d g o q u v w y z**
Start at the dot.
Turn it into _____.

Mystery Word Game with ⊂⊂

I'll help you write Magic C words. Play this game when you know all your lowercase letters.

Directions
1. Call out a **cc** or **ccc** word.
2. Spell the word.
3. Children trace **c**s to write the word.
4. Do a column a day.

⊂ ⊂ **:** ace, act, age, cat, cab, car, can, cap, do, doll, dot, gas, gap, go, got

⊂ ⊂ ⊂ **:** ago, cage, code, coat, cool, cook, dad, dog, door, good, goat, goal

LETTER STORIES

Fun stories help children remember letters that are a bit tricky. Beyond our simple verbal cues, we made up some stories that are fun to share and help make these letters memorable.

Say, "Inside **g** lives a little man named George (draw a little face in **g**)." He says, "Ohhhh, if I fall, will you catch me?" Say, "Sure, I will catch you if you fall" (turn the **g** to catch George).

Say, "**i** should be closed. If **i** is open, turn **i** into a tent. If your tent is unzipped the iguana is going to get in. If your tent is zipped (show a good **i**), the animals will mind their own business."

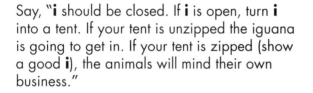

Say, "If **m** has big gaps, people will throw trash in those gaps. Don't make big gaps. Make the gaps so little, there is only room for chocolate kisses."

Say, "This is cursive **n**. It only has two humps. To remember, turn **n** into a nose and give it two nostrils."

Say, "The letter **q** is followed by **u**. Think quiet, quit, quibble, quaint, etc. At the bottom of **q**, stop and make a u-turn, then finish **q**."

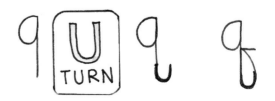

Say, "**r** doesn't have to be a difficult letter. If **r** is difficult, it's **r**'s fault. At the top of **r** we'll make a smiley face (draw a smiley face). **r** travels the line, smiles at the top and then comes down and travels the line."

Say, "When you make **s**, start with a jet take off (show arm taking off like an airplane), make a **j** (finger trace it in the air), then walk away (complete the finger trace)."

Say, "**t** should be closed. If **t** is open, turn **t** into a tent. If your tent is unzipped, the animals are going to get in. If your tent is zipped (show a good **t**), the animals will mind their own business."

Sing, "*Old McDonald Had a Farm*, **e** (at the left top side of **G** make an **e**), **i** (at the right top side of **G** make an **i**)." Finish the letter, not the song.

Say, "When you make **s**, start with a jet take off (show arm taking off like an airplane), print capital **S** (finger trace it in the air), then finish (complete the finger trace)."

Say, "I'm going to make half of a heart, you make the other half." Erase your half when the child is done and say, "Now finish the **Z**."

Posture, Paper, And Pencil Skills
PREPARING FOR PAPER AND PENCIL

When it comes to handwriting, children must be taught everything! That includes how to sit, position paper, and hold a pencil. This is the physical approach to handwriting. Sometimes it's the physical approach, not the letters and numbers, that causes a child to have trouble with handwriting. Think of it as playing a musical instrument. If you don't know how to position yourself and hold the instrument correctly, how can you play beautiful music? The same is true with writing letters and numbers. The ability to position yourself and hold your pencil correctly has a lot to do with being able to write legibly.

The important questions are:
- How do you get children to sit up while writing?
- How do you position the paper?
- What is the secret to a good pencil grip?

As you'll see in the next few pages...

Posture: Good Posture Can Be Fun

Does the furniture fit? The right size and style chair and desk affect school performance. Children don't come in a standard size! Check that every child can sit with feet flat on the floor and arms resting comfortably. Children who sit on their feet often will loose stability in their upper torso. On the following page we show you how good posture can be fun. We have a secret for getting children to stop sitting on their feet.

Paper: Place the Paper

There's a misperception that people should slant their paper to make slanted writing. Not true. In fact, we slant paper so that it fits the natural arc of the forearm. Children who slant their papers properly can write faster because the arm moves naturally with the paper.

Pencil Skills: Grasping Grip

The most important thing to understand about pencil grip is that it doesn't develop naturally; it is learned. Based on our years of experience helping children, we developed our own theories about how to develop good pencil grip habits effectively. Because children are born imitators, demonstration will lead to success.

On the next few pages, we explain fun strategies to help you teach posture, paper, and pencil skills.

GOOD POSTURE CAN BE FUN
Arms and Hands
Here are some warm-ups that children enjoy.

Push palms

Pull hands

Hug yourself tightly

Total Posture – Stomp!
Stomping is fun and really works! Students' feet will be on the floor and parallel in front of them. The arm movements make their trunks straight. The noise and chaos let them release energy, but it's under your control. When you have them stop stomping, they'll have good posture and be ready to pay attention. Use stomping a few times a day.

Directions
1. Sit down and show the children how to stomp their feet and wave their arms in the air.
2. Have them shout, "Na, na, naaah, na, na, naaah," with you as they wave and stomp.

The Stomping Game
Ask around and borrow the *Rock, Rap, Tap & Learn* CD from another teacher. Use *Stomp Your Feet*, Track 10.

Directions
1. Children push their chairs away from their desks to get ready.
2. Sing and follow along with the music and movement.

Head and Shoulders
Do this activity any time you find your children sagging.

Raise shoulders up

Pull shoulders back

Let them down

PLACE THE PAPER

Where's the paper? Most children naturally place a bowl of ice cream in front of them. However, they may lean way over in awkward positions to write. Children who put their paper in front of them and slant it properly can write faster because they position their arms naturally with the paper. You need to teach them how to place their papers appropriately. Have your students turn to page 6 in *Cursive Handwriting*, and teach them how to slant their papers appropriately for their handedness.

Children who are able to write sentences across the page are ready to tilt the paper at a slight angle to follow the natural arc of the writing hand. The correct way to tilt the paper is easy to remember (see the illustrations below). For right-handed children, put the right corner higher; for left-handed children, put the left corner higher. The writing hand is below the line of writing. This practice encourages the correct neutral wrist position.

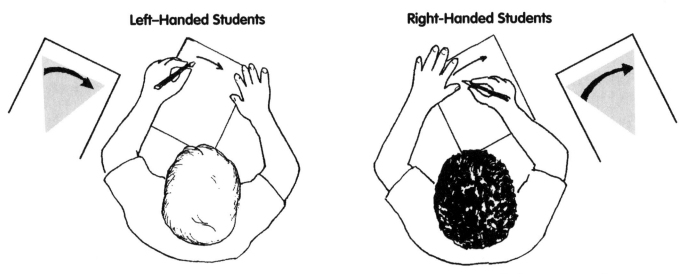

Left–Handed Students   **Right-Handed Students**

- **Left–Handed Children** tend to exaggerate the position of their papers. It helps them see their writing. For more information on left-handed children, turn to page 40.
- **Beginners** who are learning to print letters and words should place their paper straight in front of them.

Tip
- Sometimes children need reminders about how to place their paper. Draw an arrow on the bottom corner (bottom left corner for right-handed children, bottom right corner for left-handed children). Tell them to point the arrow to their belly button.

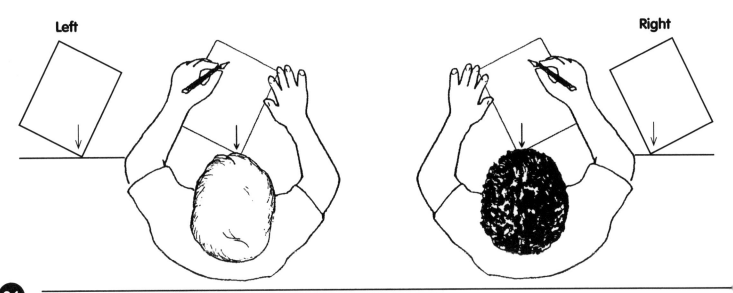

Left   **Right**

GRASPING GRIP

Educators all have questions about pencil grip. Frequently, we are asked why awkward pencil grips happen and how to correct them. We seldom hear about how to prevent them. A good pencil grip does not develop naturally. In fact, several factors affect how a child learns to hold a pencil correctly.

Below is our top 10 list of the things we often think about regarding grip:

Experiences

We develop pencil grip habits while we are young. Children who are encouraged to feed themselves have more fine motor experiences than those who are spoon fed. Children who have early self-feeding experiences may have an easier time learning how to hold their crayons and pencils.

Toys

Today's toys are very different from those with which we grew up. We should always encourage and remind parents about the non-battery operated toys because they help build hand strength.

Imitation

Children are born imitators. When they are watching you write, always demonstrate a correct grip because they tend to do as you do.

Early Instruction

Help children place their fingers. Teach preschoolers and kindergartners their finger names and finger jobs and show them how their fingers should hold writing tools.

Tool Size

Choose appropriate writing tools. We prefer small tools: Little Sponge Cubes, Little Chalk Bits, FLIP Crayons™, and Pencils for Little Hands. These tools promote using the finger tips naturally. Large tools elicit a fisted grip; small tools a more mature grip. As adults, we write with pencils that are in proportion to our hands. Shouldn't children do the same?

Timing

It is difficult to correct the grips of older children because we have to re-teach them motor patterns. Old habits die hard. Older children need time to get used to a new way of holding a pencil. It takes repetition, persistence, and practice. See page 39 of this guide.

Blanket Rules

Avoid blanket rules about pencil grip devices. Some devices may work for a child. If they are motivating and work, use them. You should save these devices as a last resort and use them for older children who understand their purpose.

Acceptance

Some awkward pencil grips are functional. If the child is comfortable and doesn't have speed or legibility issues, let it go.

Joints

We are all made differently. Some of us have joints that are more relaxed. Therefore, expect slight variations in what would be considered a standard grip (i.e., a not bent thumb, etc.). If a child is unable to use a standard grip, you may consider an altered grip as illustrated. The pencil is placed between the index and middle fingers.

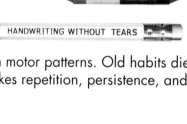

Summer

This is the perfect time to change an awkward grip. Take advantage of the child's down time to create new habits.

The Correct Grip

The standard way for children to hold their pencil is illustrated below. If you write using a grip that is different than tripod or quadropod, alter your grip for classroom demonstration.

Tripod Grip
Thumb, Index Finger, Middle Finger

Quadropod Grip
Thumb, Index Finger, Middle Finger, Ring Finger

A Note About Pencil Size

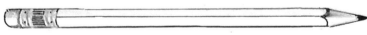

We start by using golf size pencils in kindergarten and first grade. As children gain handwriting experience, their control improves. At that time, we transition them to a standard pencil.

Cursive Warm-Ups

We created these Cursive Warm-Ups for children to test their pencil grips and practice some of the challenging strokes in cursive. Think of it as a pencil exercise. Turn to page 54 of this guide for detailed instructions. Students should do one row per day.

You can also do this page by playing Pencil Pick-Ups. Have students pick up a pencil and hold it in the air to check that they have the correct grip. Have them do one or two of the exercises and then – stop, drop their pencils, pick them up, check grips, and do a couple more exercises.

The tips shown here will help your students hold the pencil with the right combination of mobility and control. These exercises make it easy and fun for children to learn a correct pencil grip.

A-OK

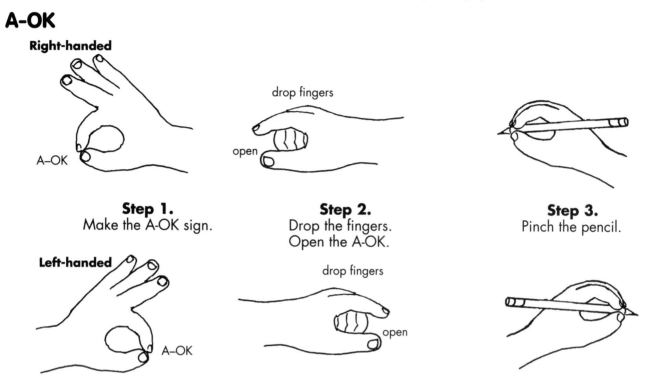

Right-handed

A–OK

drop fingers

open

Step 1.
Make the A-OK sign.

Step 2.
Drop the fingers.
Open the A-OK.

Step 3.
Pinch the pencil.

Left-handed

A–OK

drop fingers

open

Flip the Pencil Trick

Here is another method. It is a trick that someone introduced to us at a workshop. It's such fun that we love to share it. Children like to do it, and it puts the pencil in the correct position. (Illustrated for right-handed students.)

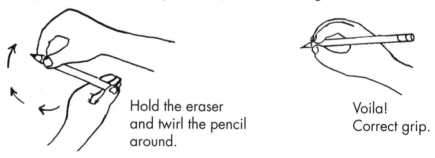

Place the pencil on table pointing away from you. Pinch the pencil on the paint where the paint meets the wood.

Hold the eraser and twirl the pencil around.

Voila!
Correct grip.

Changing Grip

There's no way of knowing for sure why non-standard grips occur. However, we believe that early instruction and good demonstration can help prevent awkward grip. Asking children to change their grips is like moving something in your house after months or years of having it in the same place. What happens? You automatically go to where the object used to be. Changing habits takes time. The same is true for pencil grip. But with grip, the adjustment takes longer. Pencil grips in older children can be changed, but it takes cooperation by the child, involvement at home and school, and a lot of time. See page 116 of this guide for ways to correct grip in three easy steps.

You may also try:
1. Using an adaptive device: With older children these devices are motivating.
2. Talking to the child: If the grip is causing discomfort, the child may be motivated to change.
3. Using an incentive program: Sometimes this motivates the child to break their habit.
4. Trying an alternate grip: Showing children something different can spark interest.
5. Making the change over summer when the non-standard grip isn't being used.

LOOKING OUT FOR LEFTIES

Many wonder if left-handed children require different instruction than right-handed children. The truth is, you instruct them the same way, with a few exceptions. Because our world typically favors the right-handed population, worksheets and letter sequence charts usually don't make special accommodations. We have tips for teaching left-handed children—tips that will prevent bad habits and make handwriting easier.

Preventing a Poor Wrist Position

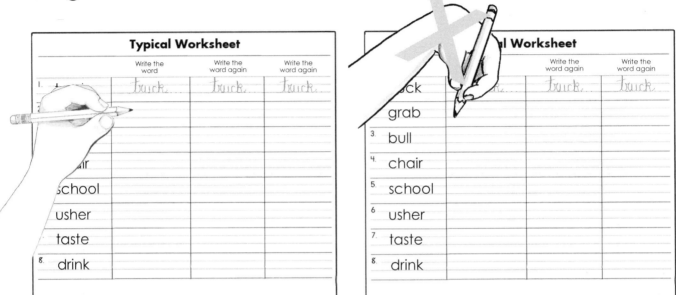

The child can't see a model.

Child accommodates but ends up in a bad position.

Many worksheets list things on just the left side. Left-handed children struggle with this format because their hand covers the thing they are attempting to copy. To accommodate their situation, some left-handed individuals will hook their wrist to see what it is they are supposed to write. After a while, the movement becomes so automatic that some children develop a natural hooked wrist pattern. This type of writing can be uncomfortable and tiring.

You can prevent this problem by photocopying the child's worksheet/workbook page and placing it to the right for the child to reference for copying.

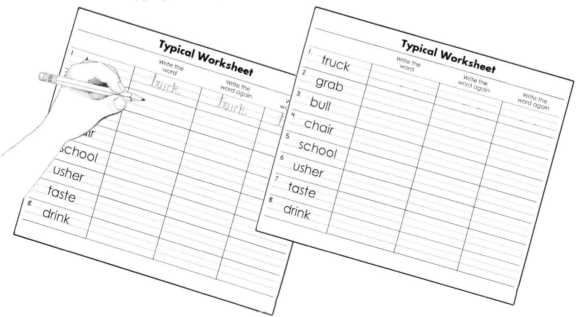

Give another copy of the worksheet to the child so the model can be seen.

Left-Hand Friendly Worksheets

When creating your own worksheets, you can make them right- and left-hand friendly in two ways:

1. Have the child copy below the model.

2. Place the word to be copied in the middle of the page.

Paper Placement

You might observe some left-handed children slanting their papers too much. They do this to prevent their wrists from hooking. You can allow them to exaggerate the slant on their papers if it doesn't cause speed or neatness trouble.

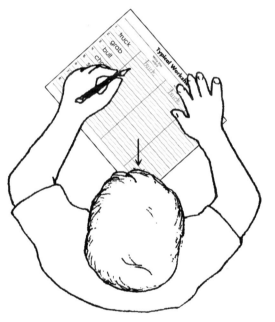

Cross Strokes

Mark arrows → for right-handed students. Mark arrows ← for left-handed students.

When writing letters and numbers, we typically travel top to bottom, left to right. At times, left-handed children will choose to pull into their writing hand from right to left. Allow left-handed children to cross by pulling into their hand. Model it for them in their workbooks.

Why Children (and Teachers) Succeed with HWT
HWT CURSIVE LETTER STYLE

HWT uses a simple, vertical cursive that is easy to learn. The HWT cursive letter style is also familiar because it looks similar to the printed letters children learned in HWT printing. HWT's continuous stroke print style prevents reversals and prepares children for a smooth transition to cursive.

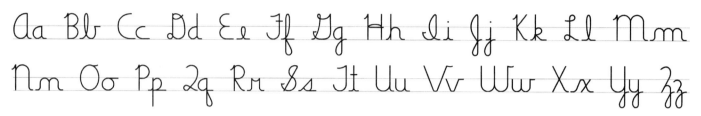

Advantages of the HWT Style

Less is more

Teaching letters with flamboyant start-up and ending strokes complicates letters and makes connecting the letters more difficult. Twenty-two letters in cursive end on the bottom line and four (**o w b v**) end on the top line. Teaching children an exaggerated bottom line start-up stroke makes it difficult for them to form connections with the four letters that do not end on the bottom line. Take a look at this style comparison and you will see why children like learning HWT cursive so much—it is easier to read and write.

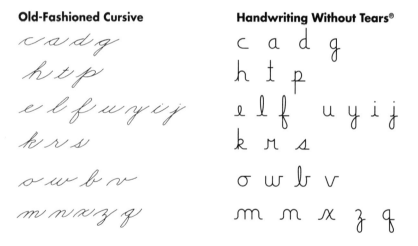

Only loopty loo when it helps you

The exaggerated beginnings and endings of letters have been removed. The curlicues, fancy loops and humps, and difficult strokes are gone. This clean and sensible style is easier for children to learn and stays neat with speed.

For example:

If you put a loop on **h** and **k**, the law of motion takes over. As the pencil curves down, it wants to keep going away. Cursive **h** and **k** often end up looking like **l** with a hump.

The HWT **h** and **k** have no loops. They are neat, easy to write, and hold together as speed increases.

The HWT *e l* and *b* have loops because the motion away from the letter is desired.

Our Slant on Slant

Here's why we remove the slant from cursive:

1. It is less intimidating to learn.
2. It is easier to write.
3. It is easier to read.
4. It leads to faster fluency.
5. It allows for personalization.

Are we breaking a rule?

Slanting to the right was a standard practice that probably developed because of old fashioned pens—thus the name "penmanship." Have you ever used an old fashioned pen, a dip or quill pen? If you have, you know that when you try to make an upstroke (from bottom to top) the pen catches, spreads, and splatters ink. Those pens are fine for vertical downstrokes but upstrokes have to be slanted. Because upstrokes are an integral part of cursive (in going from the ending place of one letter to the starting place of the next), this affected the way cursive was written. Cursive and slanting went together. But today in the era of pencils and ball point pens, it is unnecessary to slant. A vertical style is easier for teaching cursive writing. We aren't breaking a rule; we're making something easier for children.

Vertical cursive is easier to read and write.
Slanted cursive is a difficult style to learn.

Learn cursive with ease and without the slant

- The vertical line is developmentally easier than the slanted line, both to perceive and to copy. Check the notable work of Dr. Arnold Gessell on design copying.*

$$| \quad - \quad \bigcirc \quad + \quad \square \quad \triangle$$

- Vertical letters in cursive are easier for children to recognize.
- There is less to do. When learning cursive, children must master new letter formations and letter connections. There is no reason to complicate the learning process with a superfluous slant.
- Vertical cursive has a manageable accessible appearance.

* Gessell, Arnold, and others. *The First Years of Life.* New York: Harper and Row. 1940.

Slanted or vertical cursive is not a matter of correctness, it is just a matter of style. In either case, the vertical cursive is ideal for all children to learn. If a student is meant to be a slanted writer, a surprising thing will happen. The letters will naturally start to slant, and the slant will be uniform. No instruction is required. The teacher recognizes and approves of the slant as that particular child's style. For children who are vertical writers, it is not fair to impose the slant style on them because it causes many to have slow, erratic, and sloppy cursive. Most children, including most left-handed children, find vertical cursive much easier.

Tips

Because our idea about slant is unique to our method, you may hear people say our cursive is rigid and blocky. Typically, such statements come before full understanding of why we eliminated the slant. Here are a few tips to help others become comfortable with a vertical form of cursive.

1. Use the information on this page to educate others about slant.
2. Discuss personalization and fluency, see page 113 of this guide.
3. Give children permission to slant. It may be their natural style.

UNIQUE WORKBOOK FEATURES

Large Step-By-Step Illustrated Directions

It is so much easier for children to understand how to form letters if you show them how step-by-step. Other programs show a completed letter with a bunch of tiny arrows pointing the way around the letter. It is very difficult for a child to learn how to write that way. Step-by-step is the way to letter formation success.

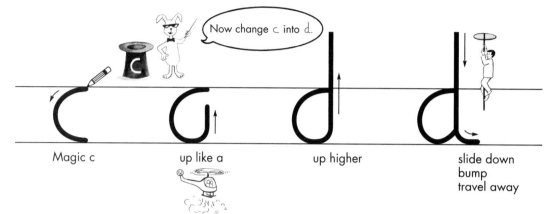

Magic c   up like a   up higher   slide down
                                                        bump
                                                        travel away

Child-Friendly Consistent Terminology

HWT's child-friendly language evolved in response to other programs' complicated letter terminology. When teaching letters to children, HWT doesn't assume they fully understand left/right orientation, clockwise/counter clockwise, or forward/backward. That complex terminology is confusing and unnecessary. HWT makes it easy by using fewer words that children already know and understand.

HWT is simple for children to comprehend.

HWT Language:
Magic c
up like a helicopter
up higher
slide down
bump
travel away

Take a look at what other programs say to form **d**:

Example 1:
Downcurve, undercurve;
slant, undercurve

Example 2:
Go overhill; retrace halfway; curve down to the bottom line; curve up right to the middle line; touch, and keep going up to the top line; retrace down, and swing up (Overhill; back, around down, touch, up high, down, and up.)

Pre-Cursive Warm-Ups Encourage Grip Practice

Pre-cursive exercises are designed to give children the opportunity to hold their pencils correctly while practicing frequently used cursive strokes. They are the perfect warm-up activity and give you the opportunity to teach and check pencil grip.

Four Simple Connections

Baseline Connections after 22 letters

Easy - Baseline to baseline connection:

Tricky - Baseline to high connection

High Connections after 4 letters: σ ɯ ƅ ν

Easy - High to high connection

Tricky - High to low connection

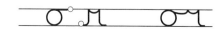

Copy Just One Model at a Time

Have you seen papers or workbooks that require children to copy a letter over and over across the page? The child copies the model and then copies the copy of the model, and so on. The letters get progressively worse. It's boring. Ideally, the child should make just one letter beside each model.

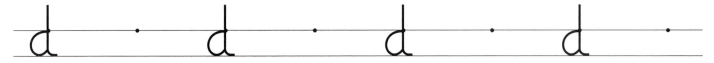

Continuous Meaningful Review

Children retain skills better if they have continuous, meaningful review. That's why each new letter is used in words and sentences that emphasize practice of the new letter and help children review and practice previously learned letters.

Room to Write

When children are learning to write in cursive, they need extra room to write. Because they can't write with the precision of machines, they cram their words to make them fit into spaces that are too small. HWT workbooks give them the room they need to write.

HWT models good spacing and gives plenty of room to write, helping children develop good spacing habits.

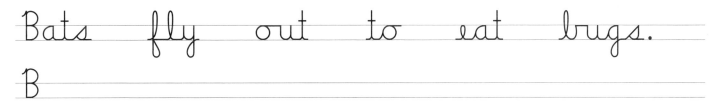

Other programs give poor spacing models and not enough room to write. Children are expected to make letters with the precision of a professional graphic designer at a keyboard.

Example 1:

Hoy likes his houseboat.

Example 2:

The Taylors started to recycle in February.

Review and Mastery

To reinforce your teaching, use the Review and Mastery section at the end of each group of cursive letters. Review and Mastery sections have three levels. Each level prepares the child for the next more challenging level. This developmentally based approach enables children to build their skills efficiently and confidently. Most important, it sets them up to write cursive neatly with speed so they are free to think about the content rather than the mechanics of what they are writing.

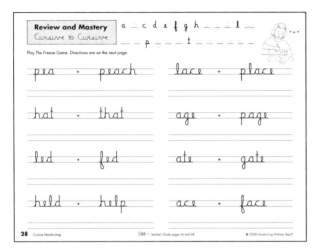

Level 1 - Cursive to Cursive

Children copy models of cursive words using recently taught letters. The correct cursive habits are reinforced by having them do word pairs that have similar parts (i.e. age/page).

Level 2 - Print to Cursive

Children look at a printed word and then have to write (translate) that word into cursive. This builds their visual memory of cursive formations.

You can play the Translate Print to Cursive game:
- Children think of words using only the letters that have been taught and then print them.
- They trade with their neighbor.
- Their neighbor has to write their printed words in cursive.

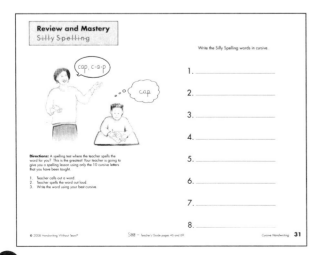

Level 3 - Oral to Cursive

This is the most advanced level before children go on to independent writing. This level entails a child hearing letters spoken and then writing that word out in cursive. This builds students' auditory memory.

Left-Hand Friendly Design

The HWT workbooks are left-hand friendly. Every page places the models so that the left-handed children can easily see the model they are copying. Lefties never have to lift their hands or place them in an awkward position to see a model. We place models on the right side so that as the left-handed child's arm covers the left aligned models, they can still see a model to copy.

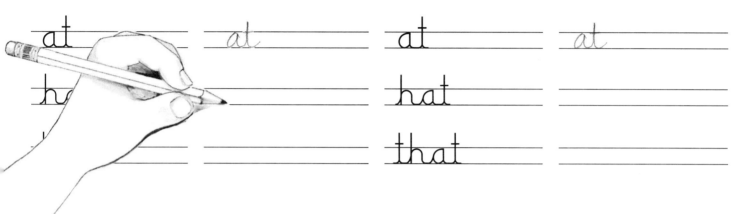

Simple Black-and-White Pages

Our workbooks have black-and-white pages that are clean and clear. We deliberately avoid the visual confusion of distracting background images, overdone colored graphics, multicolored lines, and crowded pages. These fancy effects can create visual perception difficulties for children and distract them.

The simple workbook pages keep children happy and occupied. Children who finish ahead of others can color the pictures or add drawings to the pages.

Students enjoy seeing their own writing and coloring or drawing on the pages. They like the handwritten models, which look more like their own writing. Our workbooks celebrate the child's work.

Left-to-Right Directionality

This is an exciting, unique feature of the HWT workbooks. Look at our illustrations. They promote left-to-right directionality. The zebra, game show host, koala, and other drawings are going from left to right across the page to encourage correct visual tracking and writing direction.

Fair Practice

In the workbooks, we never ask the child to copy or use a letter that has not yet been taught. The words and sentences use only the letters that the children already know. Using unfamiliar letters for instructional practice is unfair and causes children to develop bad habits.

Double Lines and Other Lines

With so many lines and so many styles, children need paper that will prepare them for it all. HWT Double Lines teach children to place letters correctly and naturally. With just two lines, children understand quickly how to place letters. Small letters fit in the middle space. Tall letters go into the top space. Descending letters go into the bottom space. Later students can apply that philosophy to other styles of paper they'll get in school. We also give them practice with other lines along the way.

Take a look at space.

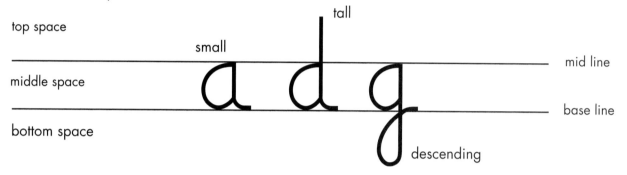

Line Generalization: Success on All Paper Styles

Throughout *Cursive Handwriting*, we provide activities for children to experience different types of lined paper. Practice using simple double lines makes it easy for students to succeed on any style of paper.

Line Generalization Success!

This child's sample shows line transition skills from HWT double lines to papers with single lines.

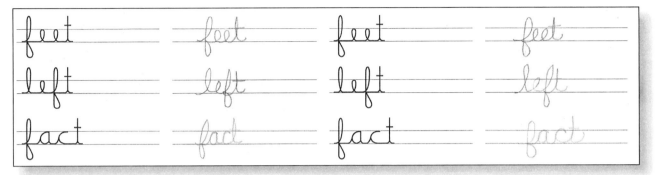

The guests danced. The guests sang.

The guests danced and sang.

The night sky sparkled. The night sky shone brightly.

The night sky sparkled and shone brightly.

The staff announced dinner. The staff served the guests.

The staff announced dinner and served the guests.

Once a year our family camps out.
We learn early to love the earth.

Paper Quality

Who would have thought that the quality of paper could affect handwriting. We tested all kinds of paper and we know good paper when we see it. Our handwriting paper is selected based on the following qualities:

1. **Writability** – This is referred to as tooth. When paper has good tooth, you can actually hear the pencil. Paper with tooth gives children feedback and assists with control. Smooth paper doesn't have tooth. It is hard to write on.

2. **Erasability** – Nothing is worse than paper that won't erase or paper that wrinkles and tears. Sturdy paper withstands erasing.

3. **Opacity** – We have the thickest sheets with the most opacity to reduce the amount of see through.

4. **Brightness** – Our paper is white. This paper helps a child's work stand out.

Cursive Handwriting
WHAT'S IN THE WORKBOOK

Cursive Handwriting uses a two-page spread to introduce new letters. The letter teaching page is on the left. The right side gives word and sentence practice using only the letters that have been taught. Review and Mastery pages at the end of each letter group give children a chance to develop their command over new letters. Activity pages provide review and practice opportunities, reinforcing important language arts skills.

Letter and Word/Sentence Pages

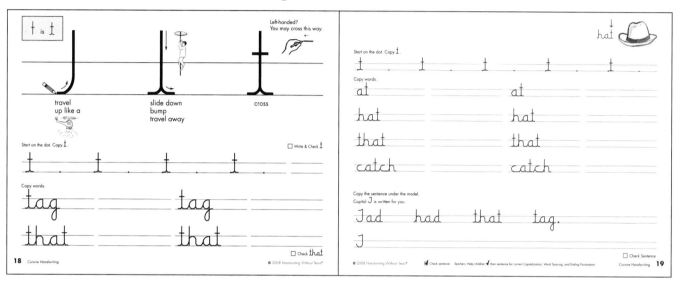

- Pages show large step-by-step instructions for letter formation.
- ☑ Check letter and ☑ Check word teach children to self-edit their work.
- Newly taught letters are immediately incorporated in word practice.

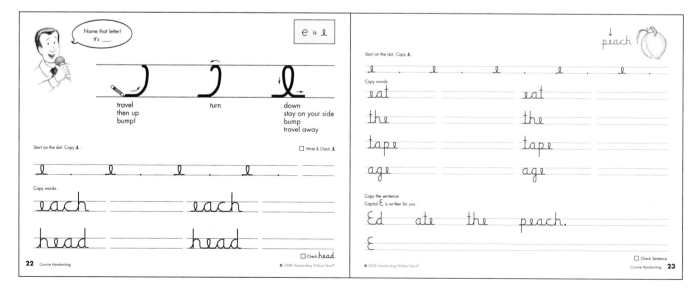

- Newly taught letters are used in practice sentences.
- Good spacing is modeled.
- ☑ Check Sentence teaches children self-editing skills.

Review and Mastery

Review and Mastery
Cursive to Cursive

Play The Freeze Game. Directions are on the next page.

pea + peach

lace + place

hat + that

age + page

led + fed

ate + gate

held + help

ace + face

28 Cursive Handwriting

Review and Mastery
Print to Cursive

flag → flag

Directions: Translate – Not Spanish, French, or Chinese. This is just translating a printed word into cursive.

1. Translate the printed words to cursive.

Total Translating –

1. Think of words that use only the letters that have been taught.
2. Write them out in print.
3. Then translate the printed word into cursive. (You can also swap books with a friend so you can translate each other's words.)

Translating

1. the
2. hat
3. help
4. feet

Total Translating

5.
6.

30

Review and Mastery
Silly Spelling

cap, c-a-p

cap

Directions: A spelling test where the teacher spells the word for you? This is the greatest! Your teacher is going to give you a spelling lesson using only the 10 cursive letters that you have been taught.

1. Teacher calls out a word.
2. Teacher spells the word out loud.
3. Write the word using your best cursive.

Write the Silly Spelling words in cursive.

1.
2.
3.
4.
5.
6.
7.
8.

Cursive Handwriting **31**

- Review and Mastery builds fluency.
- There are three levels of Review and Mastery.
- Review and Mastery can be done as games.
- Review and Mastery occurs throughout the book.

Activity Pages

COMPOUND WORDS
Figure out the compound words and write the answers in cursive.

lady + bug = ladybug

sun + shine =

horse + shoe =

cat + map =

foot + ball =

arm + chair =

hand + bag =

hair + brush =

moon + light =

book + case =

door + knob =

eye + brow =

Cursive Handwriting **91**

PARAGRAPH - DRAFT AND WRITE
Paragraphs are different from poems. Poems have lines. Paragraphs have sentences. Poems have titles; paragraphs have topics. Poems are freer. They do not always have to follow punctuation rules. Poems have rhythm or meter. Paragraphs don't, but the sentences should flow together. What you just read is a paragraph.

Draft a paragraph.
1. Tell your reader what you're going to say. That's your topic.

My topic:

2. Say it. List ideas or information about your topic. Don't use complete sentences, just get down your ideas.

About my topic:

3. Tell your reader what you said in different words.

QUOTATIONS

Always do right.

Independence is happiness

学而时习之，不亦说乎.

Mark Twain 1835-1910

Susan B. Anthony 1820-1906

Confucius 551 BC - 479 BC

Mark Twain said, "Always do right."

Susan said, "Independence is happiness."

Confucius said, "To learn and to use is a joy."

94 Cursive Handwriting

- Pages reinforce other language arts activities while promoting meaningful practice.
- Children learn to write sentences, poems, dates, letters, and days of the week.
- Children learn to write on paper with different line styles.
- Lessons are fun and engaging for students.

WHAT YOU WILL TEACH...

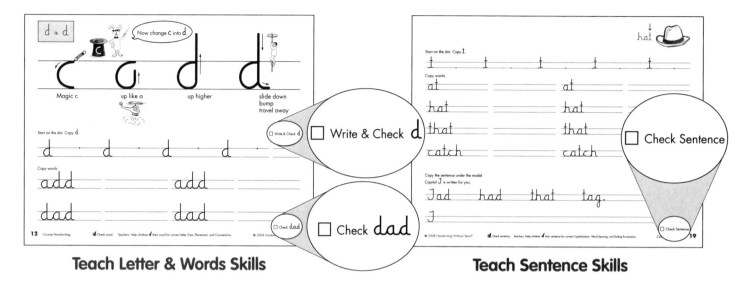

Teach Letter & Words Skills

Teach Sentence Skills

Letter Skills

Children need to know exactly how to make letters. Teach them and tell them.
Use page 5 of *Cursive Handwriting* to explain what's expected when students write letters.

1. Start correctly.
2. Do each step.
3. Bump the lines.

When you check students' workbooks, explain what they did right and help them correct any mistakes. After you have done this a few times, they'll begin to self-check with confidence.

Word Skills

There are three steps to writing words well. As you check their words, remind your students of these three important word skills.

1. Make letters the correct size.
2. Place letters correctly – tall, small, or descending.
3. Connect letters correctly.

Play the Connection Inspection on page 28 of this guide. When your students learn all the connections the activity gets more challenging and fun.

Sentence Skills

Sentences must:

1. Start with a capital.
2. Put space between words.
3. End with . ? or !

With very clear and simple expectations, children know what to do and how to do it well.

...AND HOW THEY WILL CHECK

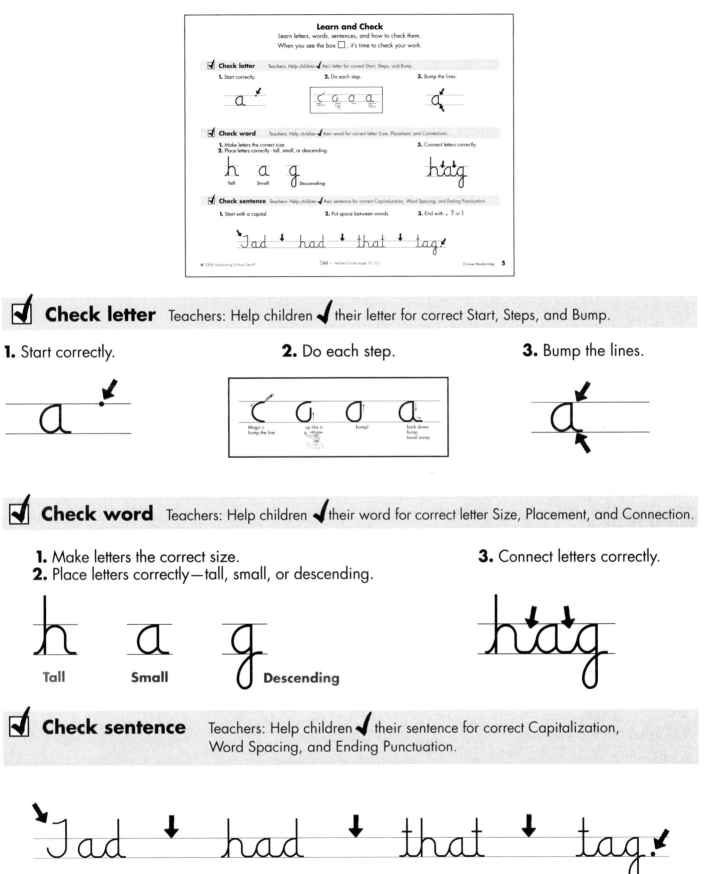

☑ **Check letter** Teachers: Help children ✔ their letter for correct Start, Steps, and Bump.

1. Start correctly.

2. Do each step.

3. Bump the lines.

☑ **Check word** Teachers: Help children ✔ their word for correct letter Size, Placement, and Connection.

1. Make letters the correct size.
2. Place letters correctly—tall, small, or descending.

3. Connect letters correctly.

Tall   **Small**   **Descending**

☑ **Check sentence** Teachers: Help children ✔ their sentence for correct Capitalization, Word Spacing, and Ending Punctuation.

CURSIVE WARM-UPS

Pre-Cursive Exercises

Prepare in the Air

Are they ready to connect letters? Teachers prepare students for the first cursive connections by making arm motions in the air. As they pretend to scoop sand and put it on a pile, they'll learn how to change directions in a stroke. Here's how:

- Children stand and put the **left hand** out to the left side.
- They scoop up the sand.
- They put the sand on top of a pile.

The scooping motion (under curve) naturally changes into a piling motion (over curve) as children pretend to scoop and pile sand.

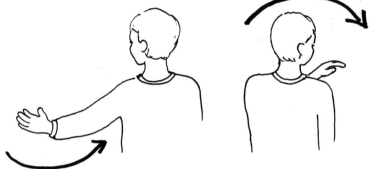

Prepare on Paper

Now have them do it with pencils using the Cursive Warm-Ups on page 7 of the workbook. The ability to change directions during a stroke is essential for making the first cursive connections. This strategy prepares students for the first cursive lessons.

Under to over

This exercise prepares for *cc* and connecting to letters *a d g o* and *q*.

This exercise prepares children for their first group of cursive letters and words. When children can complete the undercurve to overcurve exercise, they are ready to begin learning the **c** to **c** connection as well as other **c**-based connections. The **c** to **c** connection is essential for writing words that begin or contain **c**-based letters (**c a d g o q**). How many words can you think of that have a **c** to **c** connection?

Up and down retrace

This exercise helps children prepare for letters *i t u p h k*.

Up and down loop

This exercise helps children prepare for letters *b f l*.

Descending loop

This exercise helps children prepare for letters *g j y*.

These pre-cursive exercises help children prepare for important strokes required in cursive.

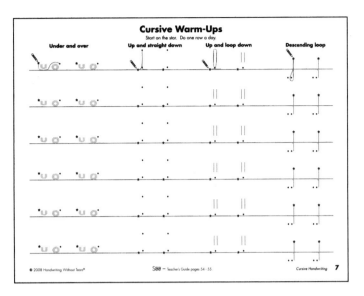

Tell them...

This is cursive warm-ups, and we have four different exercises to get ready for cursive. These warm-ups have some target practice and some running around the cones.

How do I teach this?

At the board: Draw a single baseline and then a large version of each exercise.
Demonstrate how to do each exercise.
– Wait for students to trace and then copy.
– Encourage students to help and show each other how to do the exercises.

1. Under to over

Changing directions during a stroke is necessary for cursive. The very first lesson, joining **c** to **c** requires changing from an under curve (like a smile) to an over curve (like a rainbow).

2. Up and straight down

Careful retracing makes for neat cursive, especially for the high frequency letter **t**.
Start on the dot. Touch dots as you go up and down. Then go away.

3. Up and loop down

Making neat loops for letter **l** requires a good start, a good turn, and a good return. Start on the dot. Touch the next dot and go up on the line. Turn and follow the line down to the dot. Then go away.

4. Descending loop

Making a neat descending loop is important for **g j** and **y**.
Go straight down. Turn and come up between the dots. Go to the corner and away.

A version of this page for photocopying can be found at **www.hwtears.com/click**. These exercises should be mastered before moving forward with cursive instruction.

Multisensory Activity – MAGIC C BUNNY

The Magic C Bunny helps you teach **c**-based lowercase letters **a d g o q**. The Magic C Bunny puppet will bring your lessons to life.

What does the Magic C Bunny do?
- He changes letter **c** into new letters. That's the magic trick.
- He plays Mystery Letter and Voice games.
- He makes learning fun.
- He creates a good Magic c habit for **a d g o** and even **q**.

Multisensory Activities
Music and Movement
Borrow the *Rock, Rap, Tap & Learn* CD from a kindergarten, first, or second grade teacher and have fun with the *Magic C Rap*, Track 17. This song is a great way to get your students engaged and excited about Magic c letters.
- Introduce Magic **c** while playing the *Magic C Rap*.
- Teach children to sing the chorus:

  Magic c, c for a d and g
  Magic c, c for a d and g
  Magic c, c for a d and g
  And before you're through do o and q

- Introduce the song before demonstrating Magic c letters on the board. Use the Voices activity and have Magic C Bunny whisper which voices your class should use into your ear.

Make the Magic C Bunny

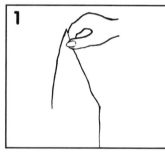

1

Open paper napkin. Hold by one corner.

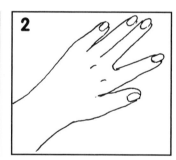

2

Spread index and middle fingers apart.

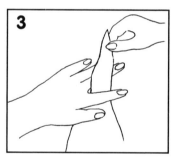

3

Pull corner between your index and middle fingers. (First ear)

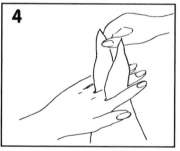

4

Take the next corner. Pull corner between your middle and ring fingers. (Second ear)

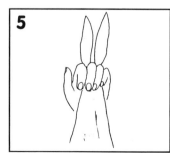

5

Fold fingers into palm.

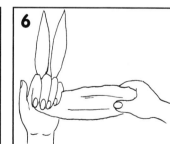

6

Pull napkin out to side.

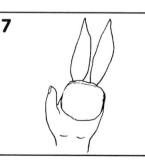

7

Wrap napkin over fingers and tuck into hand.

8

Add the face with a pen. It's a bunny! You may slip the bunny off your fingers and give it to a child. Tape or staple the napkin to hold it.

Teach

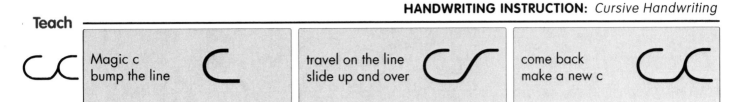

| Magic c
bump the line | travel on the line
slide up and over | come back
make a new c |

Get Started Say, "Turn to page 8. This is the Magic C Bunny. He'll help us start cursive. Cursive is connected handwriting. Watch me write cursive **c** and connect it to another **c**."

Multisensory Activities

Music and Movement
Use the *Rock, Rap, Tap & Learn* CD, *Magic C Rap*, Track 17. See page 56 of this guide.

Wet–Dry–Try
Use the Blackboard with Double Lines. See page 24 of this guide.

Finger Trace Models Step-by-Step

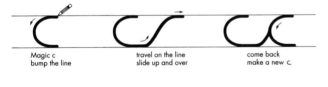

Magic c
bump the line

travel on the line
slide up and over

come back
make a new c

Say the step-by-step directions **c** to **c** while children finger trace each step.

Copy and Check c

☐ Write & Check C

Demonstrate **c**, saying the step-by-step directions. Children watch, then copy **c**s.
☑ Check letter: start, steps, bump

Tips

- This is the first page in the workbook where we do ☑ Check letter. Teach the concept and components (start, steps, bump) thoroughly. See page 52 of this guide for more information.
- If the **c** to **c** connection is difficult, have students practice the scoop to pile strokes in the air. Start at the left with a scooping stroke and slide up and over to make a piling stroke.
- If **c** is too skinny (ᕀ), tell students to begin **c** by traveling back on the top line before going down to make **c**.
- If **c**s are too close (ᕀᕀ), have students write **c**, then travel away on the line before they start the next **c**.
- Show students that cursive capital C is the same as lowercase, just bigger.

| a | Magic c bump the line | C | up like a helicopter | G | bump! | D | back down bump travel away | a |

Get Started   Say, "Turn to page 10. Watch me write cursive **a** on the double lines. I make it like this. Cursive **a** is like printed **a**, but it travels away at the end."

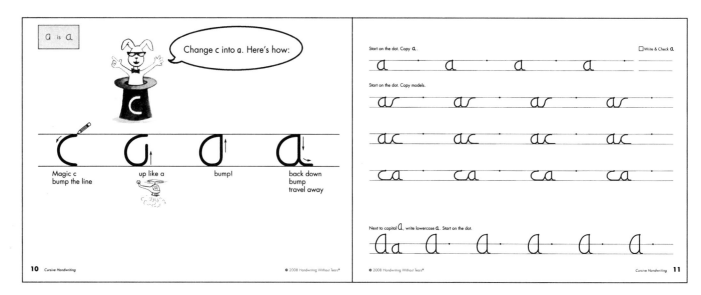

Multisensory Activities

Imaginary Writing
Use a laser and trace letter **a** on an easel. Children can follow along in the air. See page 27 of this guide.

Voices
Demonstrate **a** on the board using the Voices activity. See page 29 of this guide.

Finger Trace Models Step-by-Step

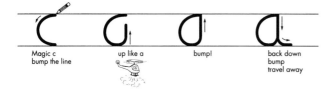

Say the step-by-step directions for **a** while children finger trace each step.

Copy and Check a

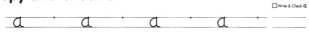

Demonstrate **a**, saying the step-by-step directions. Children watch, then copy **a**s.
☑ Check letter: start, steps, bump

Copy a to c

Demonstrate **a** to **c**.
Children watch, then copy.
(Copy other connections.)

Tips
- Teach students to travel on the line after each letter.
- If students are ending with an extravagant finishing stroke ∿, they will struggle to connect many letters. Have them make a small ending on the line.
- Show students that capital cursive 𝒜 is the same as lowercase, just bigger.

Teach

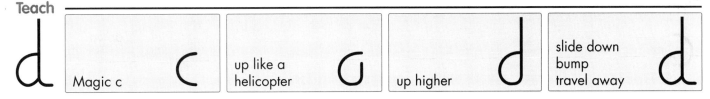

| | Magic c | up like a helicopter | up higher | slide down bump travel away |

Get Started Say, "Turn to page 12. Watch me write cursive **d** on the double lines. I make it like this. Cursive **d** is like printed **d**, but it travels away at the end."

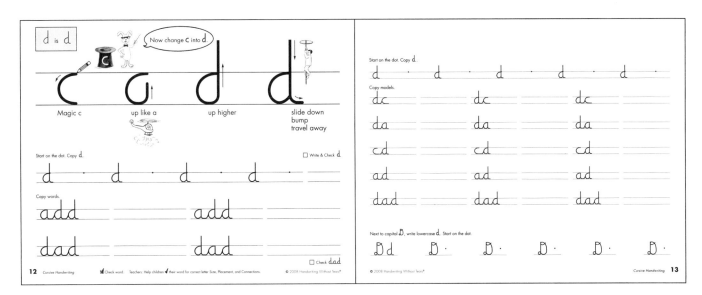

Multisensory Activities

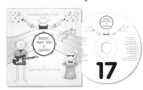

Music and Movement
Use the *Rock, Rap, Tap & Learn* CD, *Magic C Rap*, Track 17. See page 56 of this guide.

Imaginary Writing
Use *My Teacher Writes* to demonstrate **d**. See page 26 of this guide.

Finger Trace Models Step-by-Step

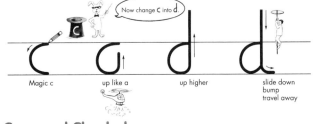

Magic c   up like a   up higher   slide down bump travel away

Say the step-by-step directions for **d** while children finger trace each step.

Copy and Check d

☐ Write & Check d

Demonstrate **d**, saying the step-by-step directions. Children watch, then copy **d**s.
☑ Check letter: start, steps, bump

Copy and Check Words with d

☐ Check dad

Demonstrate **dad**.
Children watch, then copy.
☑ Check word: size, placement, connections

Tips
- This is the first page in the workbook where we do ☑ Check word. Teach the concept and components (size, placement, connections) thoroughly. See page 52 of this guide for more information.
- If the down line slides away (𝒹) , tell students to hang onto the line with the pencil until it bumps the line.
- Point out that cursive capital 𝒟 looks like printed capital D.

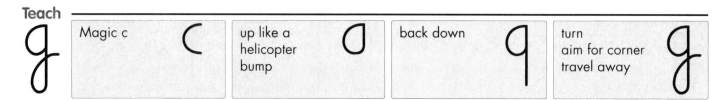

| | Magic c | C | up like a helicopter bump | Q | back down | q | turn aim for corner travel away | g |

Get Started Say, "Turn to pages 14. Watch me write cursive **g** on the double lines. I make it like this. It's easy to connect **g** to other letters. Watch me connect **g** to **a**."

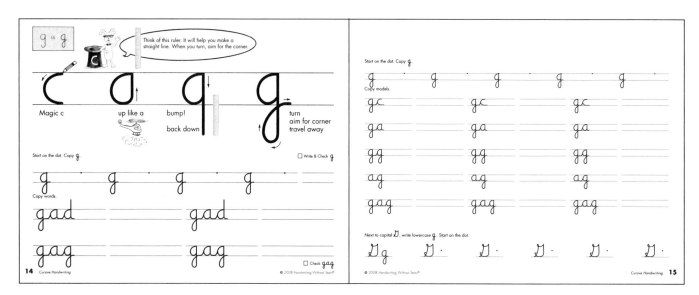

Multisensory Activities

17

Music and Movement
Use the *Rock, Rap, Tap & Learn* CD, *Magic C Rap*, Track 17. See page 56 of this guide.

Letter Story
See page 32 of this guide.

Finger Trace Models Step-by-Step

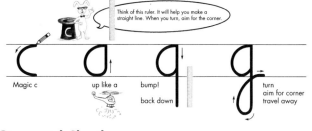

Say the step-by-step directions for **g** while children finger trace each step.

Copy and Check g

Demonstrate **g**, saying the step-by-step directions. Children watch, then copy **g**s.
☑ Check letter: start, steps, bump

Copy and Check Words with g

Demonstrate **gag**.
Children watch, then copy.
☑ Check word: size, placement, connections

Tips
- Tell students that cursive capital 𝒢 doesn't look like anything else.
- If **g** is too curvy (𝓰) , have students go down with a ruler-straight line.
- If the turn of **g** is too big 𝓰, have students slow down. Imagine a car turning in the street; make a tight turn.

Mystery Letter Game with CC

I'll help you change the second c into a, d, or g.

Directions

1. With colored pencil or pen, trace over the model CC and wait at the end.

2. Listen. Your teacher will randomly call out a d or g.

3. Change the second C into the letter that your teacher calls out.

4. Do a column a day.

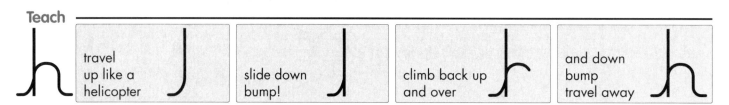

travel
up like a
helicopter

slide down
bump!

climb back up
and over

and down
bump
travel away

Get Started   Say, "Turn to page 16. This is cursive **h**. It looks like printed **h**, but it starts on the baseline. I make it like this."

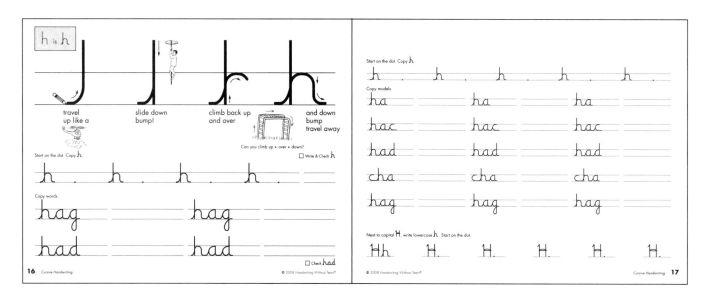

Multisensory Activities

Wet–Dry–Try
Use the Blackboard with Double Lines.
See page 24 of this guide.

Imaginary Writing
Follow the Ball and air write
h. See page 27 of this guide.

Finger Trace Models Step-by-Step

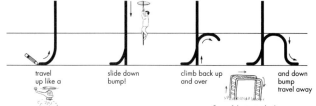

travel
up like a

slide down
bump!

climb back up
and over

and down
bump
travel away

Can you climb up + over + down?

Say the step-by-step directions for **h**
while children finger trace each step.

Copy and Check h

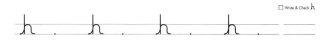

Demonstrate **h**, saying the step-by-step directions.
Children watch, then copy **h**s.
☑ Check letter: start, steps, bump

Copy and Check Words with h

Demonstrate **had**.
Children watch, then copy.
☑ Check word: size, placement, connections

Tips
- The letter **h** is the first letter that starts on the baseline.
- Encourage careful line tracing to avoid loops (𝒽) and gaps (𝓁𝓇).
- Point out that cursive capital H looks like printed capital H.

Teach

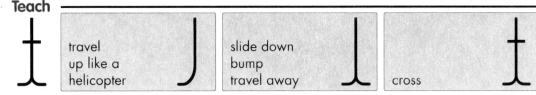

| travel up like a helicopter | slide down bump travel away | cross |

Get Started   Say, "Turn to page 18. This is cursive **t**. It looks like printed **t**, but it starts on the baseline. I make it like this. Cross **t** like this → if you're right-handed, and ← if you're left-handed."

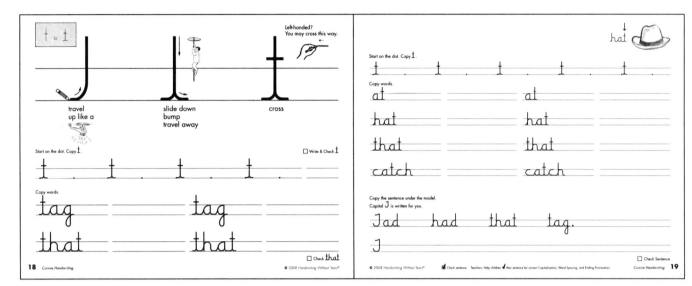

Multisensory Activities

Letter Story
See page 33 of this guide.

Finger Trace Models Step-by-Step

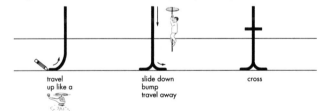

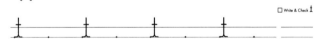

travel up like a

slide down bump travel away

cross

Copy and Check t

Copy and Check Words with t

Copy and Check Sentence with t

Tad had that tag.

T

Imaginary Writing
Use a laser and trace letter **t** on an easel. Children can follow along in the air. See page 27 of this guide.

Say the step-by-step directions for **t** while children finger trace each step.

Demonstrate **t**, saying the step-by-step directions. Children watch, then copy **t**s.
☑ Check letter: start, steps, bump

Demonstrate **that**.
Children watch, then copy.
☑ Check word: size, placement, connection

Demonstrate **Tad had that tag.**
Emphasize capitalization, word spacing, and period.
☑ Check sentence: capital, spaces, end

Tips
- Wait until the end of the word to cross **t**.
- This is the first page in the workbook where we do ☑ Check sentence. Teach the concept and components (capital, spaces, end) thoroughly. See page 52 for more information.
- Tell students that cursive capital J doesn't look like anything else.

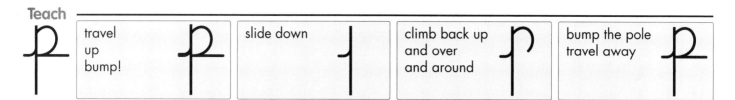

| | travel up bump! | | slide down | | climb back up and over and around | | bump the pole travel away |

Get Started Say, "Turn to page 20. Cursive **p** looks like printed **p**, but it starts on the baseline and ends by traveling away. Watch me. I make it like this."

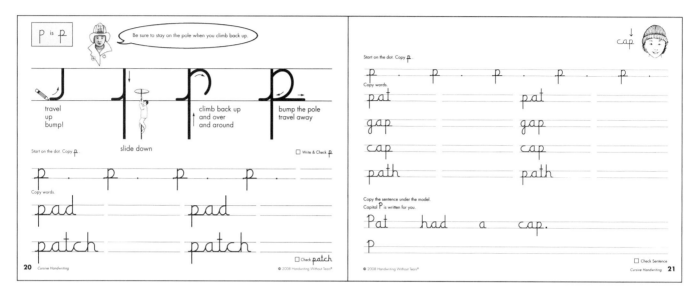

Multisensory Activities

Voices
Demonstrate **p** on the board using the Voices activity. See page 29 of this guide.

Imaginary Writing
Use a laser and trace letter **p** on an easel. Children can follow along in the air. See page 27 of this guide.

Finger Trace Models Step-by-Step

travel up bump!   slide down   climb back up and over and around   bump the pole travel away

Say the step-by-step directions for **p** while children finger trace each step.

Copy and Check p

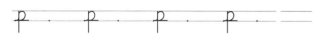

Demonstrate **p**, saying the step-by-step directions. Children watch, then copy **p**s.
☑ Check letter: start, steps, bump

Copy and Check Words with p

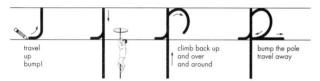

Demonstrate **patch**.
Children watch, then copy.
☑ Check word: size, placement, connections

Copy and Check Sentence with p

Demonstrate **Pat had a cap.**
Emphasize capitalization, word spacing, and period.
☑ Check sentence: capital, spaces, end

Tips

- If **p** develops a loop (ℓ), have students slide straight down and trace back up.
- Show students that cursive capital P looks like printed capital P and like lowercase cursive p.

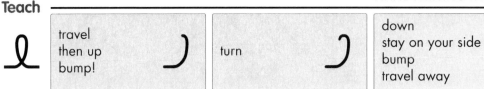

| ℓ | travel
then up
bump! |) | turn | ℐ | down
stay on your side
bump
travel away | ℓ |

Get Started Say, "Turn to page 22. Can you name that letter? It's cursive **e**. Watch me write it on the double lines. I make it like this."

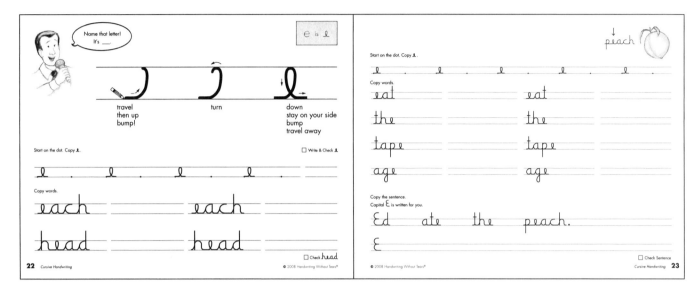

Multisensory Activities

Wet–Dry–Try
Use the Blackboard with Double Lines.
See page 24 of this guide.

Imaginary Writing
Follow the Ball and air write **e**.
See page 27 of this guide.

Finger Trace Models Step-by-Step

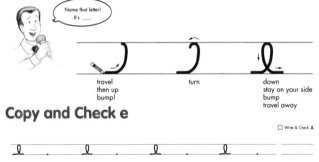

Say the step-by-step directions for **e**
while children finger trace each step.

Copy and Check e

Demonstrate **e**, saying the step-by-step directions.
Children watch, then copy **e**s.
☑ Check letter: start, steps, bump

Copy and Check Words with e

Demonstrate **head**.
Children watch, then copy.
☑ Check word: size, placement, connections

Copy and Check Sentence with e

Demonstrate **Ed ate the peach.**
Emphasize capitalization, word spacing, and period.
☑ Check sentence: capital, spaces, end

Tips

- The letter **e** is the first cursive letter that doesn't look like the printed letter.
- Tell students that cursive capital ℰ looks like a rounded printed capital E.

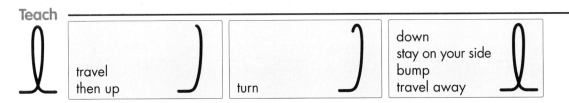

| l | travel then up | $)$ | $)$ | turn | $)$ | down stay on your side bump travel away | l |

Get Started Say, "Turn to page 24. How about this letter? Do you know what it is? It's cursive **l**. Watch me write cursive **l** on the double lines. I make it like this."

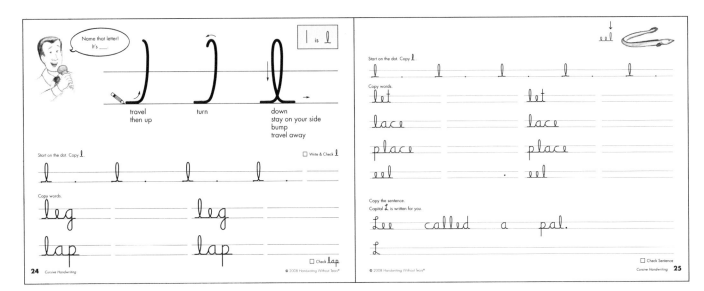

Multisensory Activities

Voices
Demonstrate **l** on the board using the Voices activity. See page 29 of this guide.

Imaginary Writing
Use *My Teacher Writes* to demonstrate **l**. See page 26 of this guide.

Finger Trace Models Step-by-Step

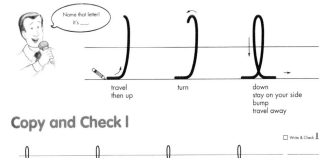

Say the step-by-step directions for **l** while children finger trace each step.

Copy and Check l

Demonstrate **l**, saying the step-by-step directions. Children watch, then copy **l**s.
☑ Check letter: start, steps, bump

Copy and Check Words with l

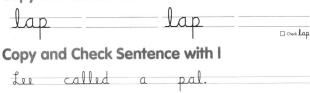

Demonstrate **lap**.
Children watch, then copy.
☑ Check word: size, placement, connections

Copy and Check Sentence with l

Demonstrate **Leo called a pal.**
Emphasize capitalization, word spacing, and period.
☑ Check sentence: capital, spaces, end

Tips
• Start **l** just like **t**. At the top, make a sharp turn and go down beside the line.
• Tell students that cursive capital **L** looks like a rounded printed capital L.

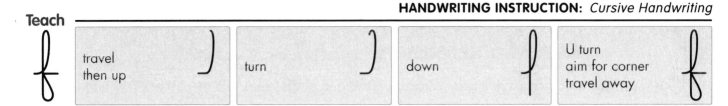

| | travel then up | | turn | | down | | U turn aim for corner travel away | |

Get Started Say, "Turn to page 26. Here's another letter that doesn't look like print. It's cursive **f**. Cursive **f** is special. It's a tall letter and also a descending letter."

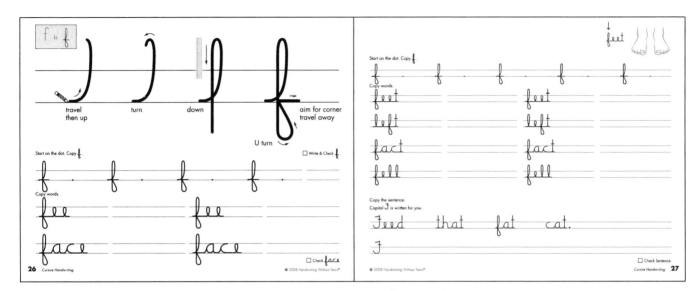

Multisensory Activities

Wet–Dry–Try
Use the Blackboard with Double Lines.
See page 24 of this guide.

Imaginary Writing
Use a laser and trace letter **f** on an easel. Children can follow along in the air.
See page 27 of this guide.

Finger Trace Models Step-by-Step

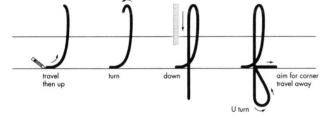

Say the step-by-step directions for **f** while children finger trace each step.

Copy and Check f

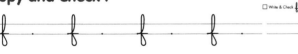

Demonstrate **f**, saying the step-by-step directions. Children watch, then copy **f**s.
☑ Check letter: start, steps, bump

Copy and Check Words with f

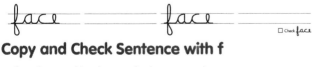

Demonstrate **face**.
Children watch, then copy.
☑ Check word: size, placement, connections

Copy and Check Sentence with f

Demonstrate **Feed that fat cat.**
Emphasize capitalization, word spacing, and period.
☑ Check sentence: capital, spaces, end

Tips
• Teach students to make a sharp u-turn at the bottom of **f**.
• Tell students that cursive capital **F** doesn't look very much like anything else.

Review and Mastery – Cursive to Cursive

HWT has a strategy for developing fluency. After this first group of ten letters and then after every three or four letters, you will use Review and Mastery activities. The first activity, Cursive to Cursive, uses word pairs to develop ease in connecting letters.

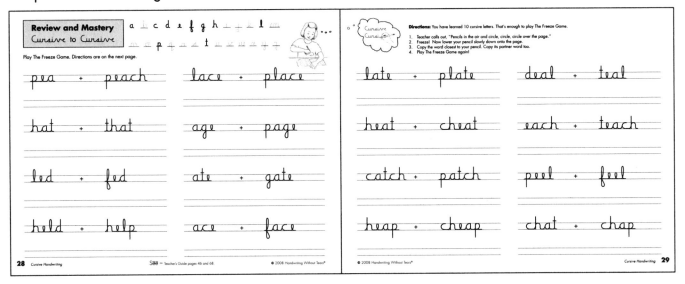

Tell them...

When people climb Mt. Everest, they stop at base camps along the way to recover and get used to the higher altitude. We are going to stop at a cursive base camp. No new letters for a few days! We are going to do review pages to get comfortable with cursive.

How do I teach this?

Introduce the Review and Mastery Cursive to Cursive pages

Explain   These words are in pairs. You will copy the first word carefully and the next word will be easy to write. This practice helps your cursive flow.

Play the Freeze Game

Say   Pencils in the air! Circle above the Review and Mastery pages.
FREEZE! Lower the pencil to land on a word.
Copy that word and the word beside it.

Continue Playing

Wait for everyone to finish copying before the next FREEZE.
Do this for two days or until all words are copied.

The FINE Print is a play on words with the name of Edith Fine, a contributor to some of the linguistic insights scattered throughout this guide. In "The Fine Print," you'll find content ranging from advanced instruction to tips that are just for fun. Edith Fine is an accomplished author of grammar and children's books.

The FINE Print   This activity is a great way to keep all students encouraged about their progress. The FREEZE game avoids the problem of comparing speed or words. All children finish the page at the same pace, and they copy different words. There is no competition.

Review and Mastery – Print to Cursive & S-I-L-L-Y S-P-E-L-L-I-N-G

Translating Print to Cursive requires more skill than just copying. Silly Spelling is the final cursive triumph. It shows an ability to remember and connect all the cursive letters that students have learned.

Translate Print To Cursive

Tell them... On this page you will translate printed words into cursive.

How do I teach this?

At the board:	Write	**flag** *flag*
	Say	This is how to translate print to cursive.
	— Supervise while students translate words.	
	Say	Challenge your neighbor to some Total Translating.
		1. Print a word that uses only your new letters: **c a d g h t p e l f**.
		2. Trade books with your neighbor.
		3. Translate your neighbor's printed word into cursive.
	— Supervise while students trade books and repeat.	

Silly Spelling Test

Tell them... Now it's time for a Silly Spelling test. It's silly because I'm going to spell the word for you, and all you have to do is write the word in cursive.

How do I teach this?

| | Choose | Appropriate words for your students. |
| | Give | Word and spelling. (That's the silly part.) Example: The first word is **cap, c-a-p.** |

Word List for c a d g h t p e l f

at	ate	aged	catch	attach	clapped	attached	tattletale
he	cat	deep	cheap	called	defaced	defeated	
	eat	each	cheat	effect	deleted	delegated	
	fad	feed	eagle	health	fetched	detached	
	get	flag	fetch	heated	flapped	placated	
	hat	glad	hatch	paddle	hatched	thatched	
	let	head	legal	patted	lactate		
	peg	heat	patch	peeled	luggage		
	tag	tape	peach	placed	patched		
	the	that	teach	teepee	pedaled		

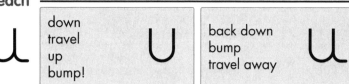

down
travel
up
bump!

back down
bump
travel away

Get Started Say, "Turn to page 32. Here's another cursive letter you can recognize! It's just like printed **u** except for the end. I make it like this."

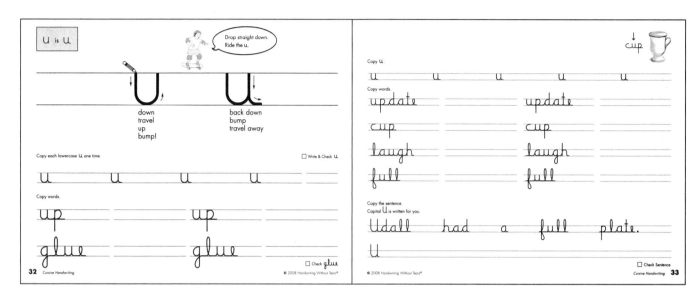

U is u

Drop straight down.
Ride the u.

down
travel
up
bump!

back down
bump
travel away

Copy each lowercase u one time.

☐ Write & Check u

Copy words.

up   up

glue   glue

32 Cursive Handwriting   © 2008 Handwriting Without Tears®   ☐ Check glue

cup

Copy u.

Copy words.

update   update

cup   cup

laugh   laugh

full   full

Copy the sentence.
Capital U is written for you.

Udall   had   a   full   plate.

u

© 2008 Handwriting Without Tears®   ☐ Check Sentence   Cursive Handwriting 33

Multisensory Activities

Connection Inspection
Form **u** words together and inspect
connections. See page 28 of this guide.

Imaginary Writing
Use *My Teacher Writes*
to demonstrate **u**.
See page 26 of this guide.

Finger Trace Models Step-by-Step

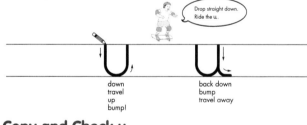

Drop straight down.
Ride the u.

down
travel
up
bump!

back down
bump
travel away

Say the step-by-step directions for **u**
while children finger trace each step.

Copy and Check u

☐ Write & Check u

u   u   u   u

Demonstrate **u**, saying the step-by-step directions.
Children watch, then copy **u**s.
☑ Check letter: start, steps, bump

Copy and Check Words with u

glue   glue

☐ Check glue

Demonstrate **glue**.
Children watch, then copy.
☑ Check word: size, placement, connections

Copy and Check Sentence with u

Udall   had   a   full   plate.

u

☐ Check Sentence

Demonstrate **Udall had a full plate.**
Emphasize capitalization, word spacing, and period.
☑ Check sentence: capital, spaces, end

Tips

• Show students that capital cursive U is the same as lowercase, just bigger.
• If **u** ends with a big tail (Ⴍ), it will look like **w**. Make a small ending on the line.

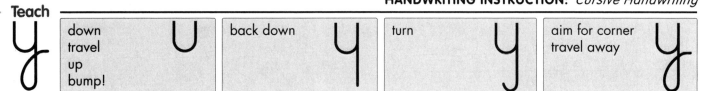

| down travel up bump! | back down | turn | aim for corner travel away |

Get Started Say, "Turn to page 34. This is cursive **y**. It's easy. Watch me write **y** on the double lines. I make it like this."

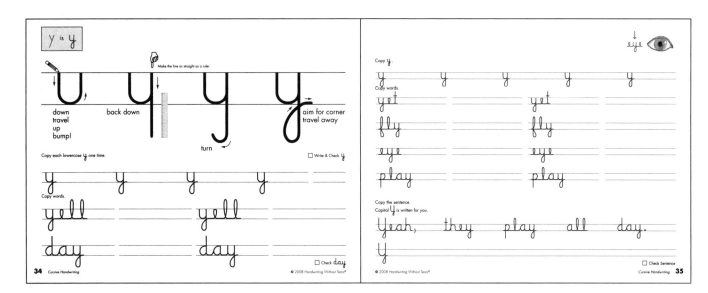

Multisensory Activities

Connection Inspection
Form **y** words together and inspect connections. See page 28 of this guide.

Finger Trace Models Step-by-Step

Copy and Check y

Copy and Check Words with y

Copy and Check Sentence with y

Imaginary Writing
Use *My Teacher Writes* to demonstrate **y**.
See page 26 of this guide.

Say the step-by-step directions for **y** while children finger trace each step.

Demonstrate **y**, saying the step-by-step directions. Children watch, then copy **y**s.
☑ Check letter: start, steps, bump

Demonstrate **day**.
Children watch, then copy.
☑ Check word: size, placement, connections

Demonstrate **Yeah, they play all day.**
Emphasize capitalization, word spacing, and period.
☑ Check sentence: capital, spaces, end

Tips
- Show students that capital cursive Y is the same as lowercase, just bigger.
- Do not use a hump (⌒y) to start y.

Teach

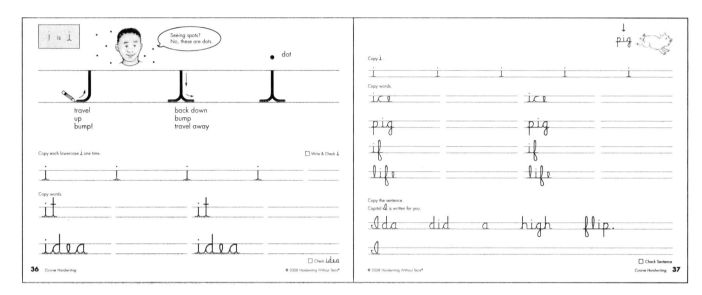

Get Started Say, "Turn to page 36. You know this letter. It's like printed **i**, but it has a different start and ending. Make it carefully so that it stays together. Watch me write **i**."

Multisensory Activities

Letter Story
See page 32 of this guide.

Voices
Demonstrate **i** on the board using the Voices activity. See page 29 of this guide.

Finger Trace Models Step-by-Step

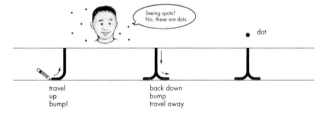

Say the step-by-step directions for **i** while children finger trace each step.

Copy and Check i

Demonstrate **i**, saying the step-by-step directions. Children watch, then copy **i**s.
☑ Check letter: start, steps, bump

Copy and Check Words with i

Demonstrate **idea**.
Children watch, then copy.
☑ Check word: size, placement, connections

Copy and Check Sentences with i

Demonstrate **Ida did a high flip.**
Emphasize capitalization, word spacing, and period.
☑ Check sentence: capital, spaces, end

Tips
- Wait until the end of a word before dotting the **i**.
- Tell students that cursive capital $\mathcal{I}$ doesn't look very much like anything else.

Teach

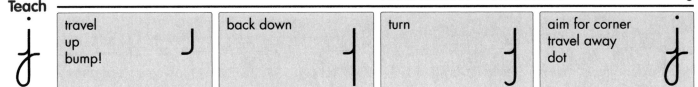

travel up bump!	back down	turn	aim for corner travel away dot

Get Started Say, "Turn to page 38. Can you recognize this letter? There's a printed **j** hiding in cursive **j**. Watch me write **j** on the double lines. I make it like this."

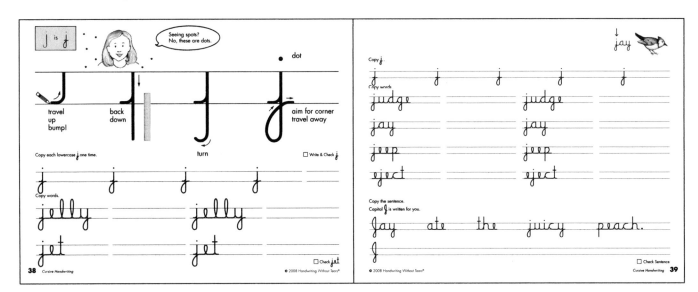

Multisensory Activities

Connection Inspection
Form **j** words together and inspect connections. See page 28 of this guide.

Imaginary Writing
Use *My Teacher Writes* to demonstrate **j**. See page 26 of this guide.

Finger Trace Models Step-by-Step

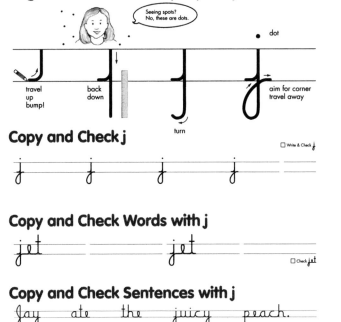

Say the step-by-step directions for **j** while children finger trace each step.

Copy and Check **j**

Demonstrate **j**, saying the step-by-step directions.
Children watch, then copy **j**s.
☑ Check letter: start, steps, bump

Copy and Check Words with **j**

jet   *jet*

Demonstrate **jet**.
Children watch, then copy.
☑ Check word: size, placement, connections

Copy and Check Sentences with **j**

Jay ate the juicy peach.

Demonstrate **Jay ate the juicy peach.**
Emphasize capitalization, word spacing, and period.
☑ Check sentence: capital, spaces, end

Tips
• Wait until the end of the word before dotting the **j**.
• Tell students that cursive capital **J** doesn't look very much like anything else.

Review and Mastery – Cursive to Cursive

Your students have four new letters: **u y i j**. Review and Mastery pages will develop fluency with them.

Tell them... You know 14 letters. The Review and Mastery words use your new letters—**u y i j**—with your old ones.

How do I teach this?

Introduce the Review and Mastery Cursive to Cursive page

Explain   These words are in pairs. You will copy the first word carefully, and the next word will be easy to write. This practice helps your cursive flow.

Play the Freeze Game

Say   Pencils in the air! Circle above the Review and Mastery page.
FREEZE! Lower the pencil to land on a word.
Copy that word and the word beside it.

Continue playing

Wait for everyone to finish copying before the next FREEZE.
Do this for two days or until all words are copied.

The FINE Print This activity is a great way to keep all students encouraged about their progress. The FREEZE game avoids comparing speed or words. All children finish the page at the same pace, and they copy different words. There is no competition.

Review and Mastery – Print to Cursive & S-I-L-L-Y S-P-E-L-L-I-N-G

Translating Print to Cursive and Silly Spelling helps students master the new letters: **u y i j**. You can modify these activities to suit your students' handwriting and academic skills.

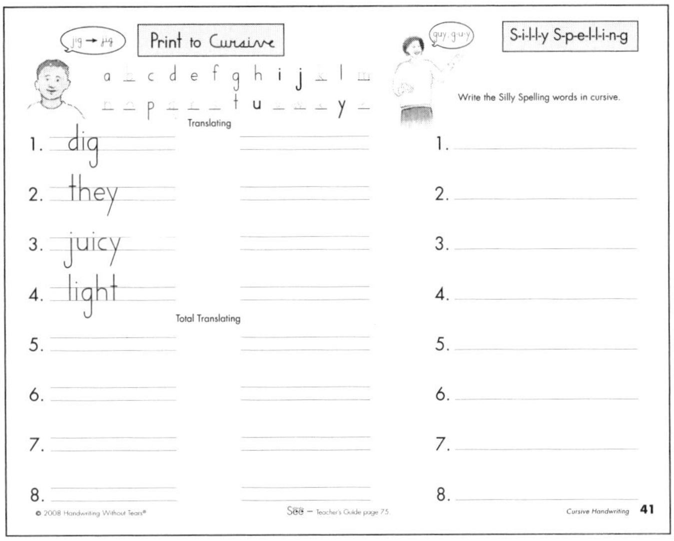

[Worksheet illustration showing "Print to Cursive" and "Silly Spelling" sections with numbered lines 1–8, words: 1. dig, 2. they, 3. juicy, 4. tight]

Translate Print to Cursive

Tell them... You will translate printed words into cursive.

How do I teach this?

At the board: Write   **jig**   *jig*
            Say   This is how to translate print to cursive.
            — Supervise while students translate words.

            Explain   Challenge your neighbor to some Total Translating.
                           1. Print a word that uses one of your new letters—**u y i j**—with the other letters.
                           2. Trade books with your neighbor.
                           3. Translate your neighbor's printed word into cursive.
            — Supervise while students trade books and repeat.

Silly Spelling

Tell them... Now it's time for a Silly Spelling test. Write the words in cursive.

How do I teach this?

            Choose   Appropriate words for your students.
            Give   Word and spelling. (That's the silly part.) Example: The first word is **guy, g-u-y.**

Word List for   c a d g h t p e l f + u y i j

up	cup	chip	alley	actual	acidity	actually	calculate	adjudicate
hi	eye	gull	eight	caught	agitate	agitated	delighted	capitulate
it	hit	itch	fifty	cloudy	applaud	athletic	difficult	delightful
	hug	jail	happy	eighty	applied	dedicate	duplicate	difficulty
	jet	life	judge	filthy	delight	dejected	dutifully	duplicated
	jug	play	laugh	guided	factual	educated	factually	telepathic
	lip	pull	piece	juggle	healthy	judicial	headlight	
	put	they	tight	little	plateau	peaceful	hopefully	
	yap	yell	uphill	taught	playful		telepathy	
	yet	yelp	yield	useful	typical			

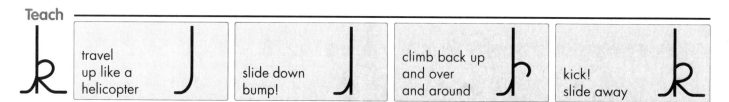

| travel up like a helicopter | slide down bump! | climb back up and over and around | kick! slide away |

Get Started Say, "Turn to page 42. This is cursive **k** with a karate kick. Watch me write cursive **k** on the double lines. This letter is fun to make."

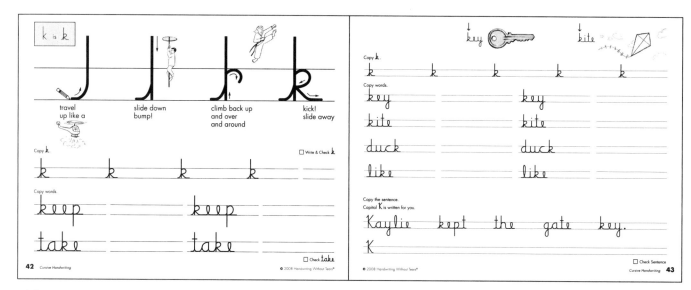

Multisensory Activities

Wet–Dry–Try
Use the Blackboard with Double Lines. See page 24 of this guide.

Voices
Demonstrate **k** on the board using the Voices activity. See page 29 of this guide.

Finger Trace Models Step-by-Step

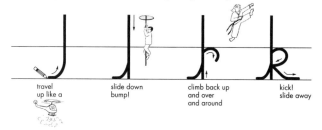

travel up like a
slide down bump!
climb back up and over and around
kick! slide away

Say the step-by-step directions for **k** while children finger trace each step.

Copy and Check k

Demonstrate **k**, saying the step-by-step directions. Children watch, then copy **k**s.
☑ Check letter: start, steps, bump

Copy and Check Words with k

Demonstrate **take**. Children watch, then copy.
☑ Check word: size, placement, connections

Copy and Check Sentences with k

Demonstrate **Kaylie kept the gate key.** Emphasize capitalization, word spacing, and period.
☑ Check sentence: capital, spaces, end

Tips
• The letter **k** is made just like the letter **h**, but with a kick.
• Show students that capital cursive K is like printed capital K.

Teach

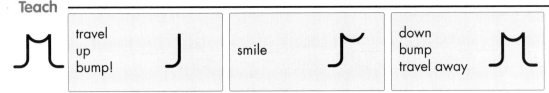

| travel up bump! | smile | down bump travel away |

Get Started Say, "Turn to page 44. This is a letter that is hard to recognize. This is cursive **r**. I want you to smile while I write it. You'll see why very soon."

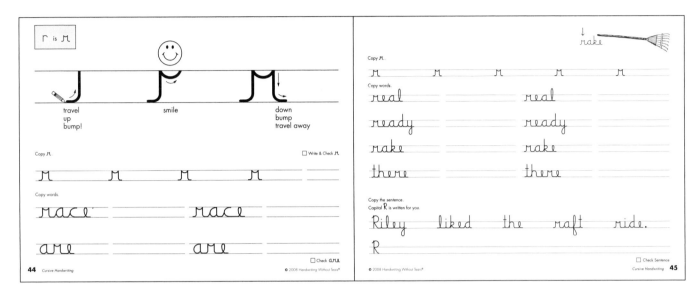

Multisensory Activities

Wet–Dry–Try
Use the Blackboard with Double Lines. See page 24 of this guide.

Letter Story
See page 33 of this guide.

Finger Trace Models Step-by-Step

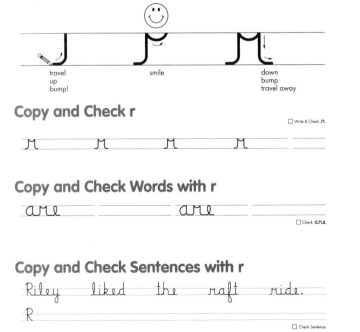

Say the step-by-step directions for **r** while children finger trace each step.

Copy and Check r

Demonstrate **r**, saying the step-by-step directions. Children watch, then copy **r**s.
☑ Check letter: start, steps, bump

Copy and Check Words with r

Demonstrate **are**.
Children watch, then copy.
☑ Check word: size, placement, connections

Copy and Check Sentences with r

Riley   liked   the   raft   ride.

Demonstrate **Riley liked the raft ride.**
Emphasize capitalization, word spacing, and period.
☑ Check sentence: capital, spaces, end

Tips
• If **r** begins or ends with a slide (⌐⌐), tell students to travel on the line, pause, go straight up, smile, and come straight down to the end of the letter.
• Capital cursive R is similar to printed R.

Teach

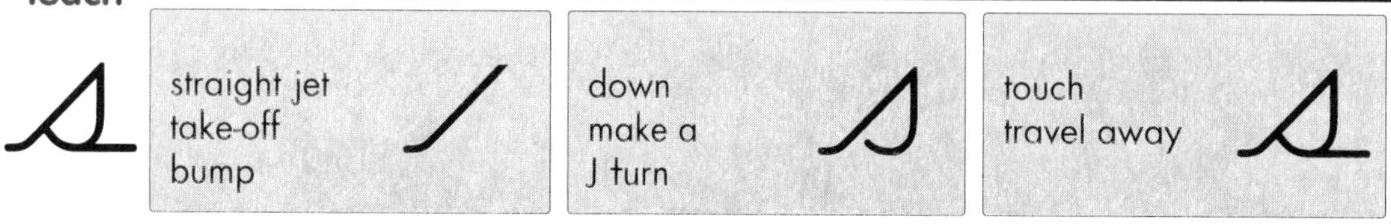

Get Started Say, "Turn to page 46. Cursive **s** does not look like printed **s**. Watch me write cursive **s** on the double lines. It's a tricky letter, but it will be easy if you make it this."

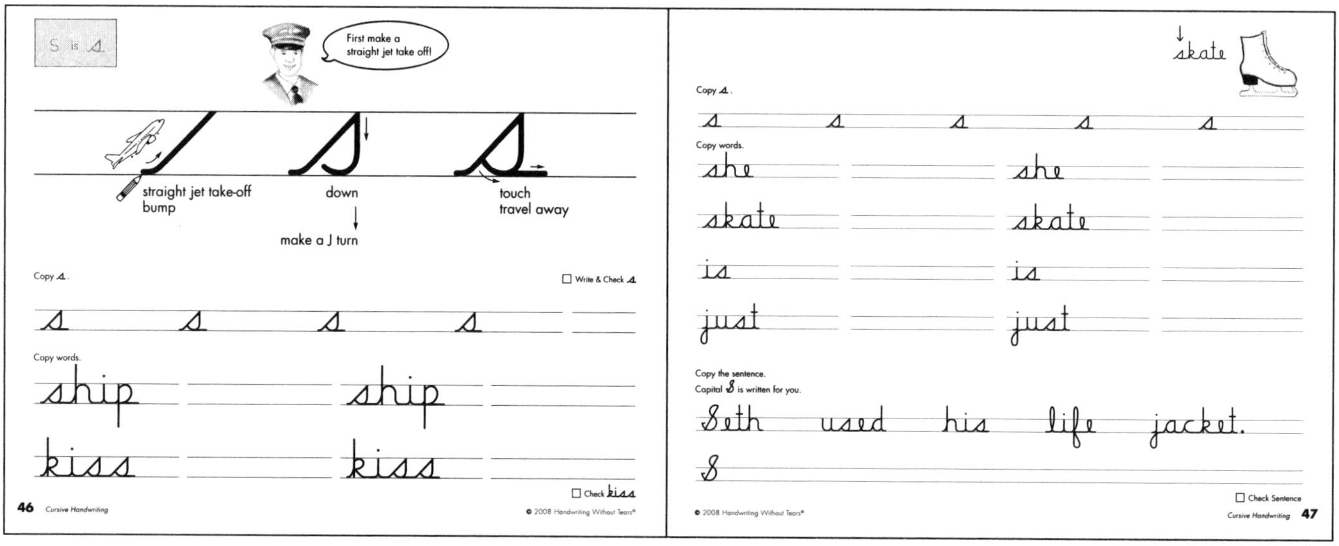
S is s
First make a straight jet take off!
straight jet take-off bump
down
make a J turn
touch travel away
Copy s.
☐ Write & Check s
Copy words.
ship ship
kiss kiss
☐ Check kiss
46 Cursive Handwriting © 2008 Handwriting Without Tears®

skate
Copy s.
Copy words.
she she
skate skate
is is
just just
Copy the sentence.
Capital S is written for you.
Seth used his life jacket.
S
☐ Check Sentence
© 2008 Handwriting Without Tears® Cursive Handwriting 47

Multisensory Activities

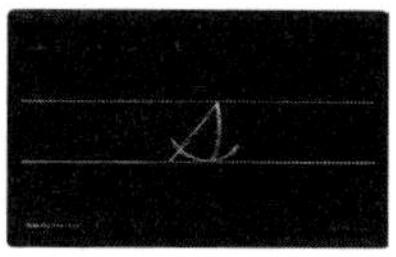

Wet–Dry–Try
Use the Blackboard with Double Lines. See page 24 of this guide.

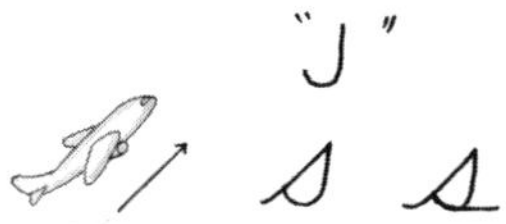

Letter Story
See page 33 of this guide.

Finger Trace Models Step-by-Step

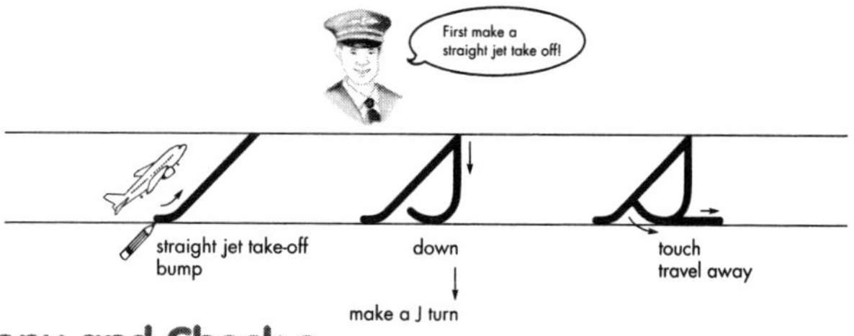

Say the step-by-step directions for **s** while children finger trace each step.

Copy and Check s

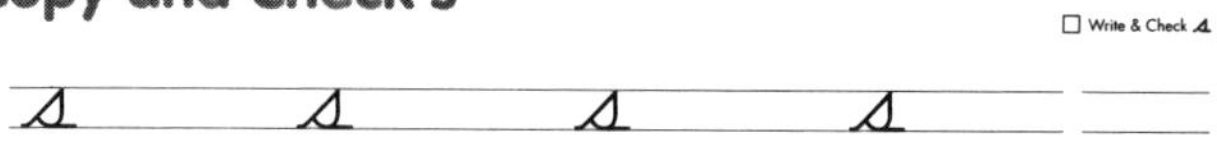

Demonstrate **s**, saying the step-by-step directions.
Children watch, then copy **s**s.
☑ Check letter: start, steps, bump

Copy and Check Words with s

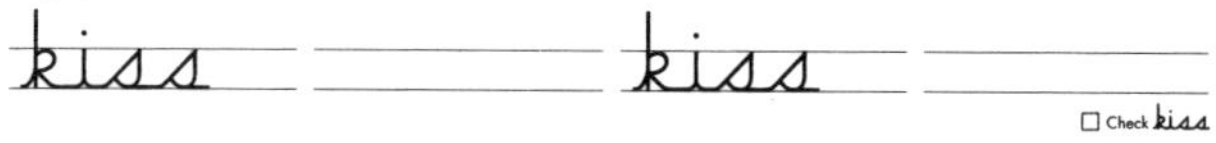

Demonstrate **kiss**.
Children watch, then copy.
☑ Check word: size, placement, connections

Copy and Check Sentences with s

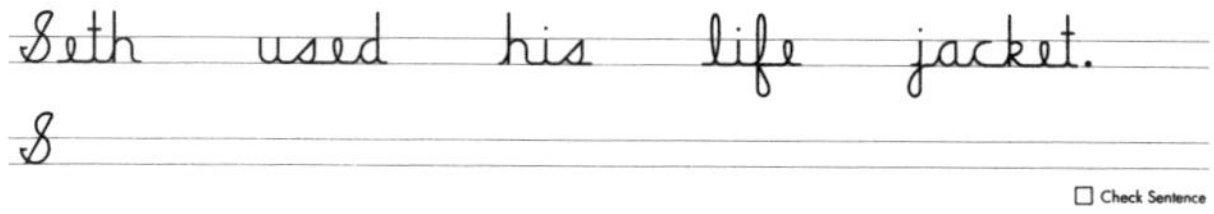

Demonstrate **Seth used his life jacket.**
Emphasize capitalization, word spacing, and period.
☑ Check sentence: capital, spaces, end

Tips

- Make the jet take-off straight. Jets don't scoop up or they'd flip over.
- If **s** balloons out (ʌ), tell students to stop at the top and drop straight down.
- Ask your students if they can see printed capital S in cursive capital S.

Review and Mastery – Cursive to Cursive

Your students have three new letters: **k r s**. Review and Mastery pages will help them develop fluency.

Tell them... You know 17 letters. The Review and Mastery words use your new letters—**k r s**—with your old ones.

How do I teach this?
Introduce the Review and Mastery Cursive to Cursive page

Explain   These words are in pairs. You will copy the first word carefully and
the next word will be easy to write. This practice helps your cursive flow.

Play the Freeze Game

Say   Pencils in the air! Circle above the Review and Mastery page.
FREEZE! Lower the pencil to land on a word.
Copy that word and the word beside it.

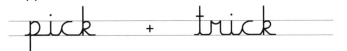

Continue playing

Wait for everyone to finish copying before the next FREEZE.
Do this for two days or until all words are copied.

Translating print to cursive and Silly Spelling help students achieve fluency with **k r s**. You can modify these activities to suit your students' handwriting and academic skills.

hers → hers	Print to Cursive	kiss, k-i-s-s
		S-i-l-l-y S-p-e-ll-i-n-g

a _ c d e f g h i j k l _
_ _ p _ r s t u _ _ _ y _
Translating

Write the Silly Spelling words in cursive.

1. his
2. here
3. lucky
4. right
Total Translating
5.
6.
7.
8.

1.
2.
3.
4.
5.
6.
7.
8.

© 2008 Handwriting Without Tears®   See – Teacher's Guide page 80   Cursive Handwriting **49**

Translate Print to Cursive

Tell them... You will translate printed words into cursive.

How do I teach this?

At the board: Write   **hers**   hers

                 Say   This is how to translate print into cursive.

               — Supervise while students translate words.

                 Explain   Challenge your neighbor

                           1. Print a word that uses one or more of your new letters—**k r s**—with the other letters listed.
                           2. Trade books with your neighbor.
                           3. Translate your neighbor's printed word into cursive.

               — Supervise while students trade books and repeat.

Silly Spelling

Tell them... On this page you will take a Silly Spelling test. Write the words in cursive.

How do I teach this?

                  Choose   Appropriate words for your students.

                  Give   Word and spelling. (That's the silly part.) Example: the first word is **kiss, k-i-s-s**.

Word List for   c a d g h t p e l f u y i j + k r s

as	are	cake	after	afraid	cracker	checkers	actresses	artificial
is	far	dish	issue	figure	fastest	clueless	architect	casualties
us	her	fish	lucky	jacket	helpful	gestured	carefully	distressed
	his	hike	price	karate	justice	kerchief	priceless	electricity
	kid	jury	rakes	packed	perfect	released	relegated	regularity
	kit	kick	ready	reject	regular	research	resurface	researched
	red	last	super	repair	repeats	selected	superstar	scattered
	rug	rack	takes	shakes	tracked	straight	surprised	subtracted
	rip	said	there	shells	ukelele	tricycle	telegraph	superficial
	she	take	tries	tissue				

Tow Truck Connections

Tow Truck letters are the only letters that do not end on the bottom line. They have a special ending—they end up high on the midline. The ending always sticks out (like a tow). The letter after a Tow Truck letter must be cranked up to the tow.

Have fun with these letters! Allow children to become the Tow Truck letters! Four children can stick their left arms to make tows. They announce their identity as Tow Truck letters.

Keep the tow up

Tow Truck letters never go down to the bottom line to join a letter. If the tow is lowered to the bottom line, the Tow Truck letter will lose its identity, creating spelling and legibility issues.

If **o** goes down to pick up a letter, it will change into a.

If **w** goes down to pick up a letter, it will change into uu.

If **b** goes down to pick up a letter, it will change into ll.

If **v** goes down to pick up a letter, it will change into u.

Easy to Tow

Some letters are easy to tow because they start on the top line. To join, simply finish the tow and begin the next letter. Easy-to-tow letters include:

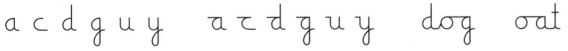

Crank up Letters

Some letters that start on the bottom line must be cranked up before they can be towed. These letters are:

Smile for the Tow

Some letters are tricky to tow. Both the tow and the letter have to change shape. Use a big smiling tow before joining to these letters:

| σ | Magic c | C | keep on going | C, | circle around | O | end with tow | σ |

Get Started Say, "Turn to page 50. Cursive **o** looks just like printed **o**, but it has a tow. The tow is part of the letter. It's always there. Watch me write cursive **o** on the double lines."

Multisensory Activities

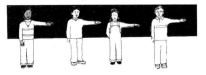

Tow Truck Activity
Cursive **o** never drops its tow or it will turn into **a**. See page 81 of this guide.

Connection Inspection
Form **o** words together and inspect connections. See page 28 of this guide.

Finger Trace Models Step-by-Step

Magic c   keep on going   circle around   end with tow

Say the step-by-step directions for **o** while children finger trace each step.

Copy and Check o

☐ Write & Check σ

σ   σ   σ   σ

Demonstrate **o**, saying the step-by-step directions. Children watch, then copy **o**s.
☑ Check letter: start, steps, bump

Copy and Check Words with o

σαr   σαr   ☐ Check σαr

Demonstrate **oar**.
Children watch, then copy.
☑ Check word: size, placement, connections

Copy and Check Sentences with o

Oscar   is   a   soccer   coach.

O   ☐ Check Sentence

Demonstrate **Oscar is a soccer coach.**
Emphasize capitalization, word spacing, and period.
☑ Check sentence: capital, spaces, end

Tips
- Make the tow straight on the σ.
- Begin the **o** on the top line to make it easy to end **o** with the tow correctly.
- Avoid any loops (σ) when ending **o** or making the tow.
- Show students that cursive capital O is like lowercase, just bigger.

Teach

⊔ℸ down and up	∪ down and up	⊔⊔ end with tow	⊔ℸ

Get Started   Say, "Turn to page 52. Printed **w** looks like a double **v**, but cursive **w** looks like a double **u** with a tow. Watch me write cursive **w**."

Multisensory Activities

Tow Truck Activity
Cursive **w** never drops its tow
or it will turn into **uu**.
See page 81 of this guide.

Connection Inspection
Form **w** words
together and inspect
connections. See page
28 of this guide.

Finger Trace Models Step-by-Step

down and up   down and up   end with tow

Say the step-by-step directions for **w**
while children finger trace each step.

Copy and Check w

☐ Write & Check ⊔ℸ

⊔ℸ   ⊔ℸ   ⊔ℸ   ⊔ℸ

Demonstrate **w**, saying the step-by-step directions.
Children watch, then copy **w**s.
☑ Check letter: start, steps, bump

Copy and Check Words with w

☐ Check ⊔ℸ⊔⊔

Demonstrate **was**.
Children watch, then copy.
☑ Check word: size, placement, connections

Copy and Check Sentence with w

Willy   saw   the   walrus.
⊔ℸ

☐ Check Sentence

Demonstrate **Willy saw the walrus.**
Emphasize capitalization, word spacing, and period.
☑ Check sentence: capital, spaces, end

Tips
• Make the tow straight on the **w**.
• Make the tow long enough so that the next letter won't be too close.
• If **w** is pointy (⊔⊓), tell students to travel on the bottom line before going up.
• Show students that cursive capital **⊔ℸ** is like lowercase, just bigger.

Teach

start with an *l* | travel and up | end with tow

Get Started Say, "Turn to page 54. Here's another Tow Truck letter. Watch me write cursive **b** in the double lines. I make it like this."

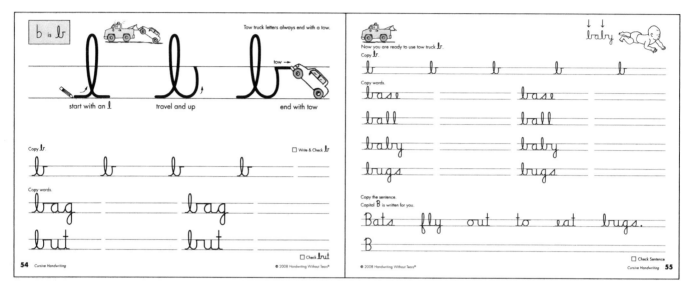

b is *b*

Tow truck letters always end with a tow.

start with an *l* — travel and up — end with tow

Copy *b*.

☐ Write & Check *b*

Copy words.

bag — *bag*

but — *but*

☐ Check *but*

54 Cursive Handwriting

© 2008 Handwriting Without Tears®

Now you are ready to use tow truck *b*.

Copy *b*.

↓ ↓
baby

b — *b* — *b* — *b* — *b*

Copy words.

base — *base*

ball — *ball*

baby — *baby*

bugs — *bugs*

Copy the sentence.
Capital B is written for you.

Bats fly out to eat bugs.

B

☐ Check Sentence

© 2008 Handwriting Without Tears®

Cursive Handwriting **55**

Multisensory Activities

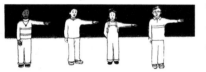

Tow Truck Activity
Cursive **b** never drops its tow or it will turn into **l**. See page 81 of this guide.

Finger Trace Models Step-by-Step

start with an *l* — travel and up — end with tow

Copy and Check b

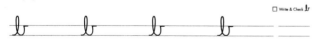

☐ Write & Check *b*

Copy and Check Words with b

☐ Check *but*

Copy and Check Sentences with b

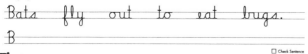

☐ Check Sentence

Connection Inspection
Form **b** words together and inspect connections. See page 28 of this guide.

Say the step-by-step directions for **b** while children finger trace each step.

Demonstrate **b**, saying the step-by-step directions. Children watch, then copy **b**s.
☑ Check letter: start, steps, bump

Demonstrate **but**.
Children watch, then copy.
☑ Check word: size, placement, connections

Demonstrate **Bats fly out to eat bugs.**
Emphasize capitalization, word spacing, and period.
☑ Check sentence: capital, spaces, end

Tips
- Make the tow long enough (*b*) so that the next letter won't be too close.
- Point out that cursive capital *B* is like printed capital B.

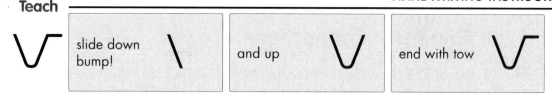

| V | slide down bump! | \ | and up | V | end with tow | V̌ |

Get Started   Say, "Turn to page 56. Watch me write cursive **v**. This is the last Tow Truck letter. The Tow Truck letters are **o w b** and **v**. The tow is part of the letter. It's always there."

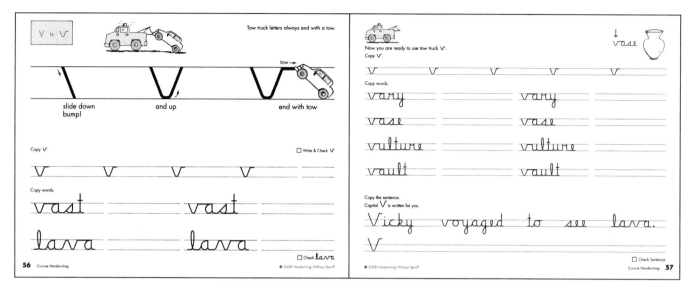

Multisensory Activities

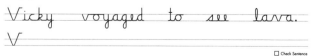

Tow Truck Activity
Cursive **v** never drops its tow or it will turn into an **u**. See page 81 of this guide.

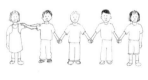

Connection Inspection
Form **v** words together and inspect connections. See page 28 of this guide.

Finger Trace Models Step-by-Step

slide down bump!   and up   end with tow

Say the step-by-step directions for **v** while children finger trace each step.

Copy and Check v

V   V   V   V

☐ Write & Check V̌

Demonstrate **v**, saying the step-by-step directions. Children watch, then copy **v**s.
☑ Check letter: start, steps, bump

Copy and Check Words with v

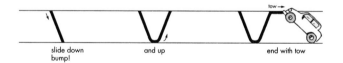

☐ Check lava

Demonstrate **lava**.
Children watch, then copy.
☑ Check word: size, placement, connections

Copy and Check Sentences with v

Vicky voyaged to see lava.

☐ Check Sentence

Demonstrate **Vicky voyaged to see lava.**
Emphasize capitalization, word spacing, and period.
☑ Check sentence: capital, spaces, end

Tips
• When the letter before **v** ends on the bottom line, climb up to start **v**.
• Show your students that cursive capital V looks like printed capital V and lowercase cursive v.

Tow Truck Connections

Get Started Say, "Turn to page 58. Before a car is towed, it has to be cranked up. The same thing happens to letters. Letters that usually start on the baseline have to be cranked up to be towed by **o w b** or **v**."

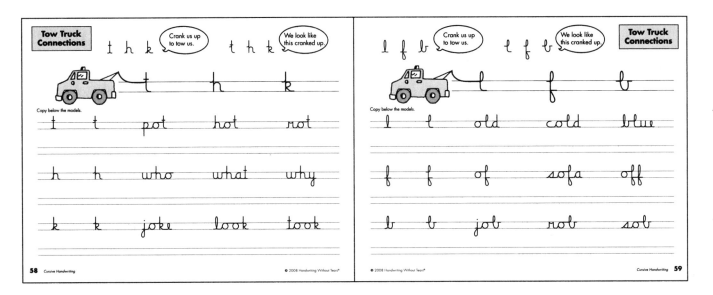

Copy t h k l f b **using Tow Truck Connections**

Demonstrate the regular letters, the cranked up letters, and words before students copy.

t t pot
h h who
k k joke
l l old
f f of
b b job

Tip

- Be sure that **f** ends on the baseline. Students often make the mistake of ending **f** higher. Practice of, off, sofa, and tofu.

Tow Truck Connections

Get Started Say, "Turn to page 60. You have learned about cranking up letters before they are towed by **o w b** or **v**. Sometimes the tow makes a big smile to make towing easier."

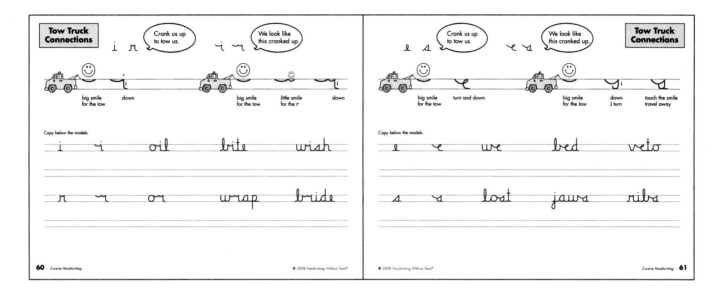

Copy i r l s Using Tow Truck Connections

Demonstrate the regular letters and the cranked up letters.
Show how to make the big smile tow after:

i i ☺ oil
r r ☺ or

Demonstrate the regular letters and the cranked up letters.
Show how to make the big smile tow after:

l e ☺ we
s s ☺ lost

Tip

• Take time to practice a few smiles.

Here are the important Tow Truck letters: **o w b v**. Review and Mastery pages help students develop fluency with this group and the other letters they already know.

Tell them... You know 21 letters. The Review and Mastery words use your new letters – **o w b v** – with your old ones.

How do I teach this?
Introduce the Review and Mastery Cursive to Cursive page
Explain These words are in pairs. You will copy the first word carefully, and the next word will be easy to write. This practice helps your cursive flow.

Play the Freeze Game
Say Pencils in the air! Circle above the Review and Mastery page.
FREEZE! Lower the pencil to land on a word.
Copy that word and the word beside it.

for   +   before

Continue playing
Wait for everyone to finish copying before the next FREEZE.
Do this for two days or until all words are copied.

Review and Mastery – Print to Cursive & S-I-L-L-Y S-P-E-L-L-I-N-G

Tow Truck letters **o w b v** are tricky to connect, but important. This page will give your students confidence in connecting those letters. You may want to do extra print to cursive or Silly Spelling on other paper.

Print to Cursive	Silly Spelling
a b c d e f g h i j k l m	Write the Silly Spelling words in cursive.
n o p q r s t u v w x y z	
Translating	
1. who _____ _____	1. _____
2. best _____ _____	2. _____
3. brave _____ _____	3. _____
4. forget _____ _____	4. _____
Total Translating	
5. _____ _____	5. _____
6. _____ _____	6. _____
7. _____ _____	7. _____
8. _____ _____	8. _____

© 2008 Handwriting Without Tears®   S88 — Teacher's Guide page 89.   *Cursive Handwriting* **63**

Translate Print to Cursive
Tell them... You will translate printed words to cursive words.

How do I teach this?

At the board: Write   **vows**   *vows*

Say   That is how to translate print into cursive.
— Supervise while students translate words.

Explain   Challenge your neighbor.
1. Print a word that uses one of your new letters **(o w b v)** with the other letters.
2. Trade books with your neighbor.
3. Translate your neighbor's printed word into cursive.
— Supervise while students trade books and repeat.

Silly Spelling
Tell them... On this page you will take a Silly Spelling test. Write the words in cursive.

How do I teach this?

Choose   Appropriate words for your students.
Give   Word and spelling. (That's the silly part.) Example: The first word is **bow, b-o-w**.

Word List for c a d g h t p e l f u y i j k r s t o w b v

be	bug	able	bride	before	aviator	baseball	advocated	apostrophe
do	bus	best	cover	busboy	baggage	bookcase	beautiful	biography
go	eve	brag	fable	forget	ecology	category	cartwheel	kaleidoscope
of	jaw	door	jewel	lawyer	hopeful	decorate	geography	psychology
or	jog	echo	table	police	hostess	elevator	periscope	scholarship
so	saw	have	vocal	review	project	football	political	screwdriver
to	vet	love	voice	revise	revised	hospital	postulate	subtracted
we	was	over	watch	school	scholar	projects	telescope	vocabulary
	who	soup	water	values	vacates	protects	tightrope	watercolor
	you	wrap	width	waiter	vehicle	trophies	waterfall	waterproof

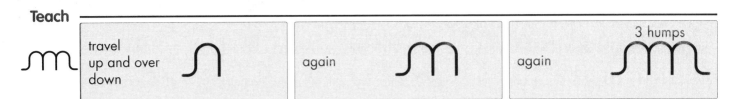

Get Started Say, "Turn to page 64. Watch me write cursive **m**. I am very careful to trace the line when I repeat the up and over part. Cursive **m** has three humps."

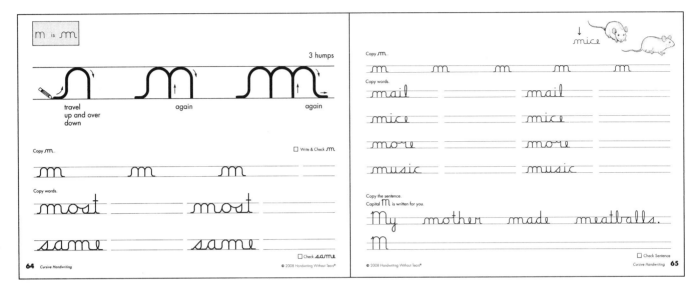

Multisensory Activities

Wet–Dry–Try
Use the Blackboard with Double Lines. See page 24 of this guide.

Letter Story
See page 32 of this guide.

Finger Trace Models Step-by-Step

Say the step-by-step directions for **m** while children finger trace each step.

Copy and Check m

Demonstrate **m**, saying the step-by-step directions. Children watch, then copy **m**s.
☑ Check letter: start, steps, bump

Copy and Check Words with m

Demonstrate **same**.
Children watch, then copy.
☑ Check word: size, placement, connections

Copy and Check Sentences with m

Demonstrate **My mother made meatballs.**
Emphasize capitalization, word spacing, and period.
☑ Check sentence: capital, spaces, end

Tips
• Teach students to walk the top line just a little for each hump.
• Cursive capital 𝓜 has two humps.

Teach

travel up and over down

again

2 humps

Get Started Say, "Turn to page 66. Cursive **n** has just two humps. You have one nose, but two nostrils. Think of that to remember two humps for cursive **n**. Watch me write **n**."

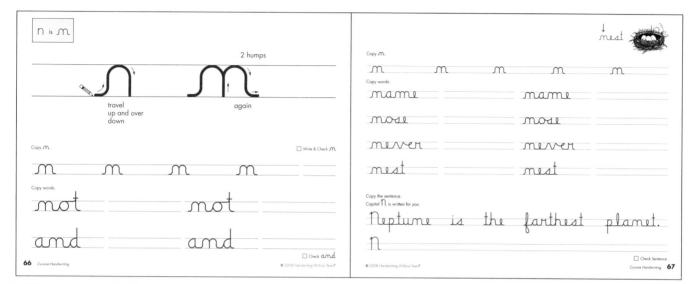

Multisensory Activities

Wet–Dry–Try
Use the Blackboard with Double Lines. See page 24 of this guide.

Letter Story
See page 32 of this guide.

Finger Trace Models Step-by-Step

2 humps

travel up and over down

again

Say the step-by-step directions for **n** while children finger trace each step.

Copy and Check n

☐ Write & Check *n*

Demonstrate **n**, saying the step-by-step directions. Children watch, then copy **n**s.
☑ Check letter: start, steps, bump

Copy and Check Words with n

and   *and*

☐ Check *and*

Demonstrate **and**.
Children watch, then copy.
☑ Check word: size, placement, connections

Copy and Check Sentences with n

Neptune is the farthest planet.
n

☐ Check Sentence

Demonstrate **Neptune is the farthest planet.**
Emphasize capitalization, word spacing, and period.
☑ Check sentence: capital, spaces, end

Tips
• Teach students to walk the top line just a little for each hump.
• Cursive capital *N* has one hump.

Teach m and n after Tow Truck letters

Cursive **m** and **n** change form when connected to a Tow Truck letter. Use the printed form of the letter after the tow.

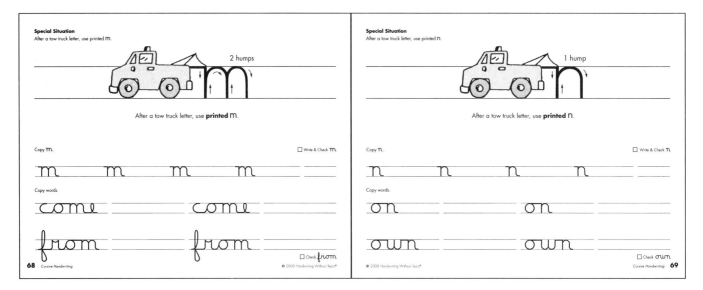

Multisensory Activity

Identify cursive m or print m quickly

Use the Blackboard with Double Lines. Write a cursive **m** and then a printed **m**. Point to each and have students say, "cursive," or "print." Then ask students to watch you write and call out "cursive," or "print" as soon as they know which one you're making. Write cursive and print **m**s randomly across the board. They'll figure out that when you start on the baseline, it'll be cursive **m**, and when you start on the midline, it'll be print **m**.

Tell them...

If you start **m** on the midline, then print **m**.
If you start **m** on the baseline, then use cursive **m**.

After cursive **o**, your pencil will be at the end of the tow, on the midline.
After **o**, print **m**.

How do I teach this?
Copy and Check m

Demonstrate **m**, saying this is printed **m**.
Children watch, then copy **m**s.
☑ Check letter: start, steps, bump

Copy and Check Words with m

Demonstrate **from**.
Emphasize using printed **m**.
Children watch, then copy words.
☑ Check word: size, placement, connections.

Modify Lesson for Letter n

Review and Mastery – Cursive to Cursive

Students know the Tow Truck letters and now have **m** and **n**. They are almost through the alphabet.

Tell them... You know 23 letters. The Review and Mastery words use your new letters **m** and **n** with your old ones.

How do I teach this?
Introduce the Review and Mastery Cursive to Cursive page

Explain   These words are in pairs. You will copy the first word carefully, and the next word will be easy to write. This practice helps your cursive.

Play the Freeze Game

Say   Pencils in the air! Circle above the Review and Mastery page.
FREEZE! Lower the pencil to land on a word.
Copy that word and the word beside it.

Continue playing

Wait for everyone to finish copying before the next FREEZE.
Do this for two days or until all words are copied.

Students now know **m** and **n**! These pages are important in developing ease in using **m** and **n** in all situations. Remember that after the Tow Truck letters, the printed style of **m** and **n** is used.

Translate Print to Cursive

Tell them... You will translate printed words to cursive.

How do I teach this?

At the board: Write   **mom**   ᴍᴏᴍ

Say   That is how to translate print into cursive.

— Supervise while students translate words.

Explain   Challenge your neighbor.

               1. Print a word that uses one of your new letters, **m** and **n**, with the other letters.

               2. Trade books with your neighbor.

               3. Translate your neighbor's printed word into cursive.

— Supervise while students trade books and repeat.

Silly Spelling

Tell them... On this page you will take a Silly Spelling test. Write the words in cursive.

How do I teach this?

Choose   Appropriate words for your students.

Give   Word and spelling. (That's the silly part.) Example: the first word is **none, n-o-n-e**.

Word List for c a d g h t p e l f u y i j k r s o w b v + m n

am	and	aunt	being	bundle	beneath	answered	confusion
an	can	band	candy	candle	general	interest	container
in	him	came	doing	making	machine	marriage	designate
me	man	down	maybe	manage	mistake	moisture	disinfect
my	may	meet	movie	motion	primate	navigate	education
no	new	most	motor	nation	promise	neighbor	newspaper
on	not	name	mouse	sample	running	thinking	primitive
	now	navy	never	saving	science	vacation	promotion
	one	sing	swing	taking	unusual	windmill	submarine
	ten	then	windy				

Teach

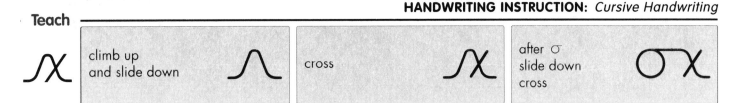

| climb up and slide down | | cross | | after ⊙ slide down cross | |

Get Started Say, "Turn to page 72. See the two ways to write cursive **x**. Watch me write cursive **x** the first way. It looks like a hill at the beginning. Watch me write **x** after cursive **o**."

[Student workbook pages 72 and 73 shown]

X is ⨯ or X

Don't cross me until you finish writing the word.

climb up slide down   cross   after ⊙ slide down cross

Copy ⨯ and X.

Copy words.

exit   exit
box   box

☐ Write & Check ⨯ and X

☐ Check box

72 *Cursive Handwriting*   © 2008 Handwriting Without Tears®

Copy ⨯ and X.

fox

Copy words.

fox   fox
extra   extra
fax   fax
tax   tax

Copy the sentence.
Capital X is written for you.

Xandra's foot was x-rayed.
X

© 2008 Handwriting Without Tears®   ☐ Check Sentence

Cursive Handwriting 73

Multisensory Activities

Wet–Dry–Try
Use the Blackboard with Double Lines. See page 24 of this guide.

Imaginary Writing
Follow the Ball and air write **x**.
See page 27 of this guide.

Finger Trace Models Step-by-Step

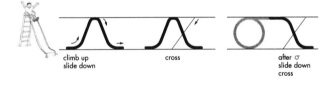

climb up slide down   cross   after ⊙ slide down cross

Say the step-by-step directions for **x** while children finger trace each step.

Copy and Check x

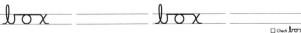

☐ Write & Check ⨯ and X

Demonstrate **x**, saying the step-by-step directions.
Children watch, then copy **x**s.
☑ Check letter: start, steps, bump

Copy and Check Words with x

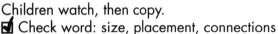

☐ Check box

Demonstrate **box**.
Children watch, then copy.
☑ Check word: size, placement, connections

Copy and Check Sentences with x

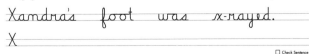

☐ Check Sentence

Demonstrate **Xandra's foot was x-rayed.**
Emphasize capitalization, word spacing, and period.
☑ Check sentence: capital, spaces, end

Tips
- When **x** comes after **o**, it begins on the top line.
- Show your students that cursive capital X looks like printed capital X.

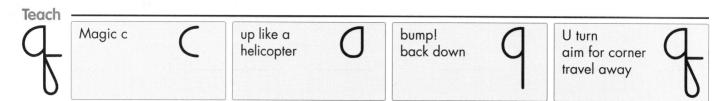

| | Magic c | | up like a helicopter | | bump! back down | | U turn aim for corner travel away | |

Get Started Say, "Turn to page 74. The Magic c bunny is back! Watch me write cursive **q**. It has a u-turn and in English, **q** is always connected to letter **u**. Watch me connect **q** to **u**."

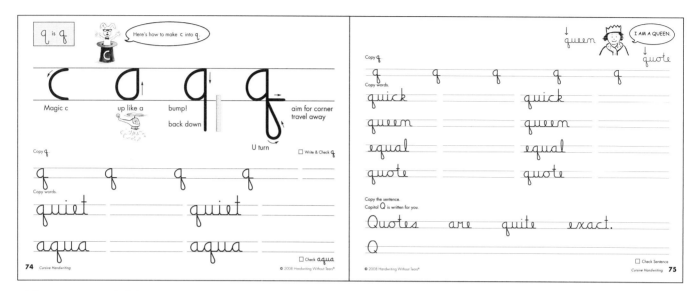

Multisensory Activities

Wet–Dry–Try
Use the Blackboard with Double Lines. See page 24 of this guide.

Letter Story
See page 32 of this guide.

Finger Trace Models Step-by-Step

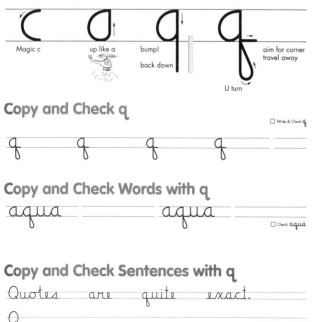

Say the step-by-step directions for **q** while children finger trace each step.

Copy and Check q

Demonstrate **q**, saying the step-by-step directions.
Children watch, then copy **q**s.
☑ Check letter: start, steps, bump

Copy and Check Words with q

Demonstrate **aqua**.
Children watch, then copy.
☑ Check word: size, placement, connections

Copy and Check Sentences with q

Demonstrate **Quotes are quite exact.**
Emphasize capitalization, word spacing, and period.
☑ Check sentence: capital, spaces, end

Tips

- Make a u-turn at the bottom of **q**. The letter **q** is always followed by **u** in **q** words.
- Capital cursive 2 is hard to remember. You may use the printed Q.

Teach

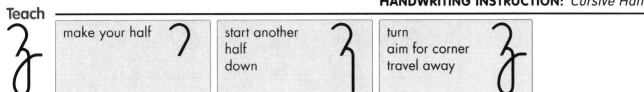

| make your half | start another half down | turn aim for corner travel away |

Get Started Say, "Turn to page 76. It's the last lowercase letter! You know all 26! Watch me write cursive **z** on the double lines. I start **z** as if I'm making half of a heart."

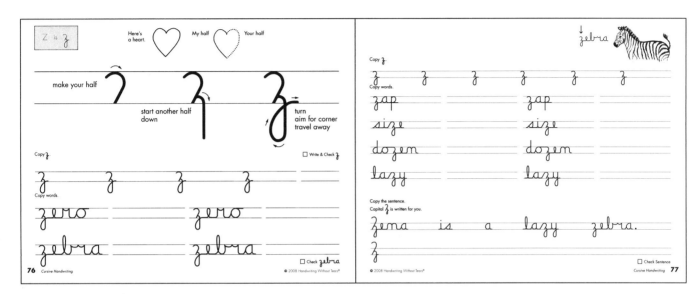

Multisensory Activities

Wet–Dry–Try
Use the Blackboard with Double Lines. See page 24 of this guide.

Letter Story
See page 33 of this guide.

Finger Trace Models Step-by-Step

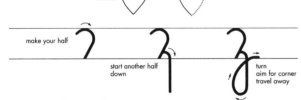

Say the step-by-step directions for **z** while children finger trace each step.

Copy and Check z

Demonstrate **z**, saying the step-by-step directions.
Children watch, then copy **z**s.
☑ Check letter: start, steps, bump

Copy and Check Words with z

Demonstrate **zebra**.
Children watch, then copy.
☑ Check word: size, placement, connections

Copy and Check Sentences with z

Demonstrate **Zena is a lazy zebra.**
Emphasize capitalization, word spacing, and period.
☑ Check sentence: capital, spaces, end

Tips
- Tell students that **z** starts with half a heart.
- Show your students that cursive capital ℨ looks like lowercase cursive ℨ, just bigger.

Review and Mastery – Cursive to Cursive

This is the final Review and Mastery activity. The workbook continues with other activities, but you may always return to Review and Mastery to polish your students' handwriting and vocabulary skills.

Review and Mastery Cursive to Cursive	a b c d e f g h i j k l m m o p q r s t u v w x y z

Play The Freeze Game.

maze + haze   box + boxer

real + realize   zeal + zealot

maze + amaze   queen + squeak

extra + extreme   quest + request

78 Cursive Handwriting   See — Teacher's Guide page 98   © 2008 Handwriting Without Tears®

Tell them… You now know all 26 letters. The Review and Mastery words use your new letters— **x q z** —with your old ones.

How do I teach this?
Introduce the Review and Mastery Cursive to Cursive page
Explain   These words are in pairs. You will copy the first word carefully and the next word will be easy to write. This practice helps your cursive flow.

Play the Freeze Game
Directions: Pencils in the air! Circle above the Review and Mastery page.
FREEZE! Lower the pencil to land on a word.
Copy that word and the word beside it.

extra + extreme

Continue playing
Wait for everyone to finish copying before the next FREEZE.
Do this for two days or until all words are copied.

Review and Mastery – Print to Cursive & S-I-L-L-Y S-P-E-L-L-I-N-G

Here are those low frequency letters. You do want to be sure that students are confident using them, especially **x**, which is used in the prefix **ex**.

Translate Print to Cursive

Tell them... You will translate print words to cursive.

How do I teach this?

At the board: Write **quiz** *quiz*

Say   That is how to translate print into cursive.

— Supervise while students translate words.

Explain   Challenge your neighbor.
1. Print a word that uses one of your new letters—**x q z**—with the other letters.
2. Trade books with your neighbor.
3. Translate your neighbor's printed word to cursive.

— Supervise while students trade books and repeat.

Silly Spelling

Tell them... On this page you will take a Silly Spelling test. Write the words in cursive.

How do I teach this?

Choose   Appropriate words for your students.
Give   Word and spelling. (That's the silly part.) Example: the first word is **box, b-o-x**.

Word List for c a d g h t p e l f u y i j k r s o w b v m n + x q z

ox	box	exit	amaze	divide	analyze	aquarium	aquaplane	aquamarine
	fax	hazy	equal	excuse	aquatic	equation	bedazzled	exhaustion
	fix	jazz	equip	exhale	equator	equality	extradite	exoskeleton
	sax	lazy	exile	exiles	example	equation	memorize	experiment
	six	quit	extra	exodus	exhaust	quackery	qualified	extraneous
	tax	whiz	fixed	prizes	exhibit	quadrant	quotation	extricated
	zip	x-ray	queen	tuxedo	extreme	quickest	quizzical	relaxation
	zoo	zany	quick	zenith	quandary	quotient	zoography	quarantine
	tag	zero	quiet	zipper	realize	zeppelin	zirconate	qualification
	the	zinc	taxes	zodiac	zoology	zwieback	zygomatic	quarrelsome

✓ Check Your Teaching

This unique strategy allows you to Check Your Teaching as you go, or Check Your Teaching at the end of it all. Because handwriting is taught through direct instruction, you can check if you did a good job teaching children letters. We have separated these mini-tests by letter group. You can give the tests to a class, but we suggest small groups or one-on-one. It's best when you can see students form their letters.

Directions:
1. On a blank sheet of paper, draw a single line.
2. Ask the child to print the word for the letter group you are checking (see below).
3. Spell the word(s) for the child.
4. Check their letters and connections.
5. If there are problems, go back and review letters with the child.

To Check: | **Child Writes:**

✓ c a d g | dad g

✓ h t p | hat cap

✓ e l f | elf

✓ u y i j | jiffy up

✓ k r s | kiss rip

✓ o w b v | we be ov

✓ m n | on am

✓ x z q | ox quiz

To give these mini tests by letter group or combined, download a Check Your Teaching worksheet at **www.hwtears.com/click**.

Capitals C a O U

These capitals are in a special teaching order to make learning easy! These cursive capitals are like the lowercase cursive letters, just bigger. You'll get two lessons in one: learning how to write the cursive capital and writing sentences that feature a variety of the capitalization rules.

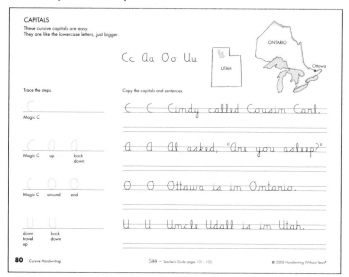

How do I teach this?

Teach C   At the board: Say   This is a very plain **C**, just like lowercase **c**.
    – Wait as students trace models.
    Write   **C**indy called **C**ousin **C**arl.
    – Wait as students copy sentence.
    Explain   Capitalize to begin a sentence. Capitalize **Cousin** before a name.
    Capitalize names.

Teach A   At the board: Demonstrate   Each step and repeat with students.
    – Wait as students trace models.
    Write   **A**l asked, "**A**re you asleep?"
    – Wait as students copy sentence.
    Explain   To write a quote you need: a comma, first quotation marks, the quote, ending punctuation, and last quotation marks.
    Capitalize to begin a sentence. Capitalize to begin a quote.

Teach O   At the board: Demonstrate   Each step and repeat with students.
    – Wait as students trace models.
    Write   **O**ttawa is in **O**ntario.
    – Wait as students copy sentence.
    Explain   Capitalize to begin a sentence. Capitalize names of cities and provinces.

Teach U   At the board: Demonstrate   Each step and repeat with students.
    – Wait as students trace models.
    Write   **U**ncle **U**dall is in **U**tah.
    – Wait as students copy sentence.
    Explain   Capitalize to begin a sentence.
    Capitalize **Uncle** before a name.
    Capitalize names of states.

Capitals V W X Y Z

These cursive capitals are like the lowercase cursive letters. You'll get two lessons in one: learning how to write the capitals and writing sentences that feature a variety of the capitalization rules.

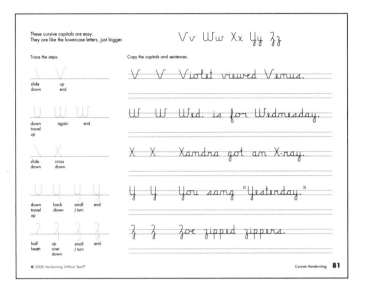

How do I teach this?

Teach V At the board: Demonstrate Each step and repeat with students.
– Wait as students trace models.
Write **V**iolet viewed **V**enus.
– Wait as students copy sentence.
Explain Capitalize to begin a sentence. Capitalize names and planets.

Teach W At the board: Demonstrate Each step and repeat with students.
– Wait as students trace models.
Write **W**ed. is for **W**ednesday.
– Wait as students copy sentence.
Explain Capitalize to begin a sentence. Capitalize days of the week.

Teach X At the board: Demonstrate Each step and repeat with students.
– Wait as students trace models.
Demonstrate **X**andra got an **X**-ray.
– Wait as students copy sentence.
Explain Capitalize to begin a sentence. Capitalize names and the word **X-ray**.

Teach Y At the board: Demonstrate Each step and repeat with students.
– Wait as students trace models.
Write **Y**ou sang "**Y**esterday."
– Wait as students copy sentence.
Explain Capitalize to begin a sentence. Capitalize song titles.

Teach Z At the board: Demonstrate Each step and repeat with students.
– Wait as students trace models.
Write **Z**oe zipped zippers.
– Wait as students copy sentence.
Explain Capitalize to begin a sentence. Capitalize names.

The FINE Print Capitalize the first, last, and important words in song and book titles.

Capitals P B R Π Μ H

These cursive capitals are easy like the print letters. They are similar to capital **P B R H** and lowercase **n m**. In cursive, they all start the same way with a short ready stroke and then a big line down.

Trace the steps. They start the same.

Copy the capitals and sentences.

P		P P Pre is a prefix.	
ready down	up around		
P	B	B B Bob backpacked in Brazil.	
ready down	up around	around again	
P	R	R R Raisa reads Russian.	
ready down	up around	slide down	
Π		Π Π Nov. is for November.	
ready down	up over down		
Μ		Μ Μ Mr. Moe met Meagan.	
ready down	up over down	one more	
H	H	H H Hey - hay are homonyms.	
ready down	down	up over	end

82 *Cursive Handwriting*   © 2008 Handwriting Without Tears®

How do I teach this?

Teach P   At the board: Demonstrate   Each step and repeat with students.
                              – Wait as students trace models.
                              Write   **P**re is a prefix.
                              – Wait as students copy sentence.
                              Explain   Capitalize to begin a sentence.

Teach B   At the board: Demonstrate   Each step and repeat with students.
                              – Wait as students trace models.
                              Write   **B**ob backpacked in **B**razil.
                              – Wait as students copy sentence.
                              Explain   Capitalize to begin a sentence. Capitalize the name of a country.

Teach R   At the board: Demonstrate   Each step and repeat with students.
                              – Wait as students trace models.
                              Write   **R**aisa reads **R**ussian.
                              – Wait as students copy sentence.
                              Explain   Capitalize to begin a sentence. Capitalize names and languages.

Teach N   At the board: Demonstrate   Each step and repeat with students.
                              – Wait as students trace models.
                              Write   **N**ov. is for **N**ovember.
                              – Wait as students copy sentence.
                              Explain   Capitalize to begin a sentence. Capitalize months of the year.

Teach M   At the board: Demonstrate   Each step and repeat with students.
                              – Wait as students trace models.
                              Write   **M**r. **M**oe met **M**eagan.
                              – Wait as students copy sentence.
                              Explain   Capitalize to begin a sentence. Capitalize titles such as Mr. and names.

Teach H   At the board: Demonstrate   Each step and repeat with students.
                              – Wait as students trace models.
                              Write   **H**ey - hay are homonyms.
                              – Wait as students copy sentence.
                              Explain   Capitalize to begin a sentence.

Capitals K T F I J D

These capitals are in a special teaching order to make learning easy, but after capital **K**, they get harder. These cursive capitals don't look like the lowercase cursive letters. They also don't look much like the printed capitals. Review the capitalization rules with each sentence.

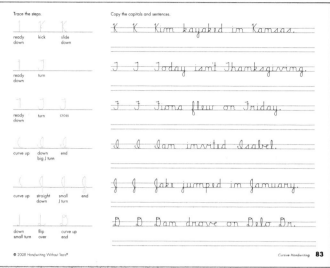

How do I teach this?

Teach K   At the board: Demonstrate   Each step and repeat with students.
  – Wait as students trace models.
  Write   ***K**im kayaked in **K**ansas.*
  – Wait as students copy sentence.
  Explain   Capitalize to begin a sentence. Capitalize the names of states.

Teach T   At the board: Demonstrate   Each step and repeat with students.
  – Wait as students trace models.
  Write   ***T**oday isn't **T**hanksgiving.*
  – Wait as students copy sentence.
  Explain   Capitalize to begin a sentence. Capitalize holidays.

Teach F   At the board: Demonstrate   Each step and repeat with students.
  – Wait as students trace models.
  Write   ***F**iona flew on **F**riday.*
  – Wait as students copy sentence.
  Explain   Capitalize to begin a sentence. Capitalize the days of the week.

Teach I   At the board: Demonstrate   Each step and repeat with students.
  – Wait as students trace models.
  Demonstrate   ***I**an invited **I**sabel.*
  – Wait as students copy sentence.
  Explain   Capitalize to begin a sentence. Capitalize names.

Teach J   At the board: Demonstrate   Each step and repeat with students.
  – Wait as students trace models.
  Demonstrate   ***J**ake jumped in **J**anuary.*
  – Wait as students copy sentence.
  Explain   Capitalize to begin a sentence. Capitalize the months of the year.

Teach D   At the board: Demonstrate   Each step and repeat with students.
  – Wait as students trace models.
  Demonstrate   ***D**an drove on **D**elo **D**r.*
  – Wait as students copy sentence.
  Explain   Capitalize to begin a sentence. Capitalize the name of a street, drive, or road.

Capitals ℒ 𝒢 𝒮 ℰ 𝒬

These capitals are in a special teaching order to make learning easy, but this is another hard group. The only easy one is **Q**, if you and your students decide to use the printed version of **Q**. Review the capitalization rules in each sentence.

Trace the steps.

Copy the capitals and sentences.

start like ɪ — down — flip
in the air — small turn — over

ℒ ℒ Lori left Lake Louise.

curve up — top like — down — end
ɪ + ɪ — big J turn

𝒢 𝒢 Georgia glided in Greece.

jet take off — print s — end

𝒮 𝒮 Sue signed Sincerely, Sue.

c in the air — c again

ℰ ℰ Ed enjoyed Europe.

half — small — flip
heart — turn — over

Q 𝒬 Quit that Quentin!

84 *Cursive Handwriting*

© 2008 Handwriting Without Tears®

How do I teach this?

Teach L	At the board:	Demonstrate	Each step and repeat with students.
		– Wait as students trace models	
		Write	**L**ori left **L**ake **L**ouise.
		– Wait as students copy sentence.	
		Explain	Capitalize to begin a sentence. Capitalize the name of a lake, river, or ocean.
Teach G	At the board:	Demonstrate	Each step and repeat with students.
		– Wait as students trace models	
		Write	**G**eorgia glided in **G**reece.
		– Wait as students copy sentence.	
		Explain	Capitalize to begin a sentence. Capitalize the name of a country.
Teach S	At the board:	Demonstrate	Each step and repeat with students.
		– Wait as students trace models	
		Write	**S**ue signed **S**incerely, **S**ue.
		– Wait as students copy sentence.	
		Explain	Capitalize to begin a sentence. Capitalize letter closings and names.
Teach E	At the board:	Demonstrate	Each step and repeat with students.
		– Wait as students trace models.	
		Write	**E**d enjoyed **E**urope.
		– Wait as students copy sentence.	
		Explain	Capitalize to begin a sentence. Capitalize the name of a continent.
Teach Q	At the board:	Demonstrate	Each step and repeat with students.
		– Wait as students trace models	
		Write	**Q**uit that **Q**uentin!
		– Wait as students copy sentence.	
		Explain	Capitalize to begin a sentence. Capitalize names.

Handwriting instruction progresses in three levels: imitation, copying, and independent writing. Fun Letter Sentences are independent writing.

FUN LETTER SENTENCES

Ⓐ B C D E F G H I J K L M
N O P Q R S T U V W X Y Z

Choose your six favorite letters. Circle them.
Now write a fun sentence to feature each letter.

A   Adam ate apples in Alabama.

© 2008 Handwriting Without Tears®   Cursive Handwriting **85**

Tell them…
You may have favorite capital letters. Perhaps you like writing them or they are special because they are in your name. On this page, you will pick a letter to start every word, or almost every word, in a sentence.

How do I teach this?

Explain   Every sentence must feature a single letter. Silly sentences are fine! You may use a different letter only if it's absolutely necessary.

At the board:

Make a Chart	**Subject**	**Verb**	**Object**	**Preposition**	**Object**
Write	Adam	ate	apples	in	Alabama.
Write	Barbara	blew	bubbles	in	Boston.

Explain   This is just one way to make up fun letter sentences. Now make up your own.
– Supervise students as they make up their own sentences.

Activity Page – Rain Forest

This is something different. It's a page to enjoy, think about, and color. The sentences are placed on the page according to the layers of a rain forest.

EMERGENT LAYER	RAIN FOREST		RAIN FOREST ANIMALS	
	Tall trees reach for the sun.		*Butterflies flit; parrots fly.*	
CANOPY LAYER	*Leaves crowd the top.*		*Monkeys howl and screech.*	
UNDERSTORY LAYER	*Tree trunks stand in the shade.*		*Snakes slither and jaguars run.*	
FOREST FLOOR	*It's dark, damp, and squishy.*		*Anteaters search for ants.*	

86 Cursive Handwriting   © 2008 Handwriting Without Tears®   © 2008 Handwriting Without Tears®   Cursive Handwriting 87

Tell them...

Rain forests are located around the world. Most of them are near the equator where it's warm and wet. Rain forests teem with life, with thousands and thousands of varieties of plants and animals. There are layers to the rainforest. Most animals live or stay in just one or two layers. Some animals never even touch the ground. They live their lives in the trees.

How do I teach this?

Talk about the design of these two pages and the layers of a rain forest.

Explain   This two-page spread has an unusual design.

1. Page 86 has sentences about the layers of the plants and trees in the rain forest. The sentences are placed in layers too. The sentence about the emergent layer is at the top. The sentence about the forest floor is at the bottom.

2. Page 87 has sentences about the animals that live in the rain forest. The sentences are in layers too. For example, the sentence about animals in the emergent layer is at the top.

Activity Page – Paragraph & Paragraph Draft

On page 88 of the workbook is a paragraph about moons, an informational paragraph about the solar system. Page 89 is an independent writing activity that will help students as they choose a topic and develop their ideas into a paragraph.

Paragraph

Tell them…

Not until man invented clear glass and learned how to grind glass did people see things that were very small or very far away. Convex and concave lenses changed what we could see. The microscope and telescope changed our vision and what we know.

How do I teach this?

Use this page to review six capitals.

At the board: Say   On this page, I want to review capitals and whether you should connect them.
Take your pencil and circle all the words with capitals. Then we'll talk about them.

Write   You   Say   **Y** ends on the baseline and the right side. Connect **Y** to **o** in **You**.
Earth's   Say   **E** ends on the baseline and the right side. Connect **E** to **a** in **Earth**.
Other   Say   **O** does not connect to the next letter.
Galileo   Say   **G** does not connect to the next letter.
Jupiter's Say   **J** ends on the baseline and the right side. Connect **J** to **u** in **Jupiter's**.
In   Say   **I** does not connect to the next letter.

– Check that the capitals are done correctly.

Paragraph Draft

Tell them…

On this page, you're going to draft ideas for a paragraph. That's a way to collect and organize your thoughts before you write.

How do I teach this?

Choose what's best for your class.

1. Children write independently.

2. Do the paragraph draft together at the board.

Discuss   Steps and develop the ideas together.
At the Board: Write   Draft of paragraph sentence by sentence:
1. Topic Sentence
2. Ideas and information
3. Restated topic sentence
– Students copy final paragraph on notebook paper.

Activity Page – Poem

This poem page follows a paragraph page. Let's compare!

POEM

<u>Words Work</u>

Some words work, they earn their keep

They make me laugh, they make me weep

They take me places I want to go

They teach me things I need to know.

90 *Cursive Handwriting*   © 2008 Handwriting Without Tears®

Tell them...
You can see that this page has a title, "Words Work," and it says POEM at the top of the page. Before you copy the poem, we are going to read the poem and compare it with the paragraph page.

How do I teach this?
Read the poem as a class. Talk about the meaning of the poem. How can words work? How do words have value?

Compare this poem with the paragraph.
At the board: Make Headings for a chart. **Poem**   **Paragraph**
             Say   This poem has a title.
             Ask   Does the paragraph have a title? No, the paragraph has a topic, not a title.

Continue filling in the chart as you compare the poem with a paragraph.

Poem	**Paragraph**
Title	Topics
Lines	Sentences
Starts at the left	Indented
Each line has its own line	Sentences share lines
Rhyme	No
Rhythm or meter	No
Ends with nothing, commas, or sometimes a . ! or ?	end with a . ? or !
–Supervise students as they copy the poem	

The FINE Print You may show your students the rhyme pattern for the poem. Use **A** for keep, **A** for weep; **B** for go, **B** for know. Words that rhyme get the same letter. When the rhyme changes, the letter changes.

Activity Page – Compound Words

Students will enjoy this page! Compound words give them confidence in writing longer cursive words.

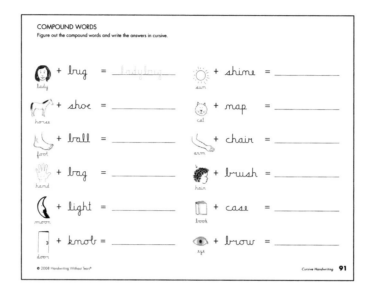

Tell them...

A compound word is made from two words. For example: lady + bug = ladybug. On this page they used pictures instead of words for the first word.

How do I teach this?

Take turns saying the words:

Students:	Picture word	
Teacher:	Cursive word	*bug*
Students:	Compound word	*ladybug*

At the board: Write **lady + bug = ladybug**

– Supervise students as they write the compound words.
– Help as needed with spelling or cursive writing.

The FINE Print Some teachers develop spelling and handwriting skills with compound words. Start a class compound word collection. Tell students to bring a compound word to school tomorrow. It's fun to add pictures too.

Activity Page – Punctuation, Dates, Greetings and Closings, and Letters

Punctuation, dates, greetings, and closings will prepare them to write the letter on the facing page.

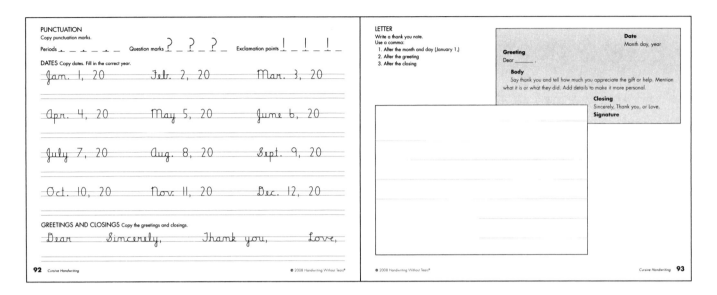

Tell them...

This is a page for practicing writing capitals and the parts of a letter: dates, greetings, and closings. They didn't fill in the year. It just says "20__." Can you guess why? They didn't know in which year we would be using this page. I want you to fill in the year for all of the dates that you copy.

How do I teach this?

Review capital formation and whether or not to connect. On the teacher's chart below "——" means don't connect.

Write	Explain	
Jan.	**J** ends on the baseline and the right side.	Connect **J**.
Feb.	——	
Mar.	**M** ends on the baseline and the right side.	Connect **M**.
Apr.	**A** ends on the baseline and the right side.	Connect **A**.
May	**M** ends on the baseline and the right side.	Connect **M**.
June, July	**J** ends on the baseline and the right side.	Connect **J**.
Aug.	**A** ends on the baseline and the right side.	Connect **A**.
Sept.	——	
Oct.	——	
Nov.	**N** ends on the baseline and the right side.	Connect **N**.
Dec.	——	
Dear	——	
Sincerely,	——	
Thank you,	——	
Love,	**L** ends on the baseline and the right side.	Connect **L**.

These famous people are here to help you teach the correct form for writing quotations.

QUOTATIONS

Always do right.

Independence is happiness.

学而时习之，不亦说乎.

Mark Twain
1835-1910

Susan B. Anthony
1820-1906

Confucius
551 BC - 479 BC

Mark Twain said, "Always do right."

Susan said, "Independence is happiness."

Confucius said, "To learn and to use is a joy."

94   Cursive Handwriting   © 2008 Handwriting Without Tears®

Tell them...

The people on this page are famous. I'll tell you a little about them now, but you will learn more about them when you're in fourth or fifth grade—maybe in college.

1. Mark Twain wrote books and gave humorous talks. Someday you will read *The Adventures of Tom Sawyer* or *The Adventures of Huckleberry Finn*. The end of his quote is funny. Here it is: "Always do right. This will gratify some people and astonish the rest."

2. Susan B. Anthony worked for years to get women the right to vote, but she died before they got it. She said, "Independence is happiness."

3. Look at the writing! Confucius was a famous Chinese philosopher. You will copy a translation. One of his famous quotes is, "A journey of a thousand miles begins with a single step."

How do I teach this?

	Explain	Quotations are a person's exact words. Quote bubbles show the words.
At the board:	Write	In cursive: Mark Twain said, "Always do right."
	Explain	Comma after said,
		First quotation marks
		Exact quote with ending punctuation
		Last quotation marks

– Supervise students as they copy the quotations.

The FINE Print We condensed the quotation from Confucious to make it fit on the page. A more accurate translation would be: "To learn, and to put to use, is that not a joy?" We're told that virtually every child in China knows this quotation and their parents do too!

HANDWRITING ADVICE
Fluency and Personalization

When children have learned letter formation and connections, they will gain speed. With speed comes fluency; with fluency comes personalization. Our handwriting style is unique to each of us. As we develop our own style, we also develop consistent patterns. Eventually it's inevitable: we will develop our own unique style.

Take a look! This child learned the HWT style of cursive!

ear / er /		*Beautiful writing! 100%*		**Spelling Words**
1. earn	1	*earn*	*earn*	*earn*
2. early	2	*early*	*early*	*early*
3. earth	1	*earth*	*earth*	*earth*
4. learn	1	*learn*	*learn*	*learn*
5. search	1	*search*	*search*	*search*
6. pearl	1	*pearl*	*pearl*	*pearl*
7. heard	1	*heard*	*heard*	*heard*

You will know that your students are gaining fluency and personalization when you start to see:
1. Speed
2. Natural flare (loops and curlicues)
3. Possible slant
4. A mixture of print with cursive

Mixing print with cursive is normal. If students start to mix their print with cursive, allow it. This style of writing is very functional and often is the way most adults write. Don't let the cart get before the horse though. If a child begins to personalize too soon, hold the child accountable for neatness and completeness.

Ease Their Minds...
Some may worry that the HWT vertical style is too simple. Our clean style actually leads children to even greater fluency and personalization—*quickly*! When you teach the most important parts of the skill (formation and connection), the other pieces (beauty and speed) come naturally. For those who fear that our cursive style is a bit too simple, remind them of what happened to the duck in the story "The Ugly Duckling"—that's our point! HWT cursive develops into a beautiful swan that can fly fast.

Identifying Handwriting Difficulties

As discussed in the beginning of this guide, your students may come with very different levels of writing proficiency. This section is especially important for those who enter your room less prepared. Think in terms of the eight skills required for speed and legibility (page 7). If you break the handwriting processes into these skills, you will be able to identify and correct difficulties more easily. Use the tips below to guide your approach when helping a child who is behind in handwriting. Often the cursive and printing skills are fine, but the physical approach to handwriting or the child's interest in self-correction may need some adjustments. If you feel the difficulty stems from something other than just a lack of instruction, consult an occupational therapist.

Below are some of the things to look for to identify where a child needs help. On the pages that follow, we include strategies for addressing the specific difficulties.

PHYSICAL APPROACH

Handedness
- Switches hands while writing
- Switches hands between activities

Pencil Grip
- Holds pencil straight in the air
- Wraps thumb around fingers
- Uses an awkward grip
- Holds pencil with an open hand

Pencil Pressure
- Breaks pencils
- Writes illegibly

Paper Placement
- Positions paper incorrectly for handedness

Posture
- Slouches in chair
- Has head on table
- Slumps

Helper Hand
- Moves paper when writing

SELF CORRECTION

Erasing/Editing
- Erases too much
- Works carelessly

PRINTING & CURSIVE SKILLS

Memory
- Misses letters or numbers in assignments
- Confuses capital and lowercase letters
- Writes unidentifiable letters/numbers

Orientation
- Reverses letters or numbers

Placement
- Places letters incorrectly
- Uses wrong lines

Size
- Makes letter size too big for grade level papers

Start
- Starts with the wrong part or on the wrong side

Sequence
- Forms letter strokes out of order

Spacing
- Puts too much space between letters and words
- Runs words together

Control
- Makes misshapen letters/numbers

Connections
- Breaks connections
- Does not start Magic c letters with **c** stroke
- Drops the tow in Tow Truck letters
- Uses awkward connections

Remediating Handwriting Difficulties

The remediation strategies here can help you correct some of the handwriting difficulties you observe. Furthermore, parents often ask teachers ways they too can assist their child. This section will give you tips and ideas to correct the handwriting difficulties that you see. It will also give you information parents are seeking.

When facilitating handwriting remediation, remember the following:

Notice what's right: Recognition of what's right is encouraging and should come before any suggestions or corrections. Limit the number of mistakes that you mark on a page. It is best to mark just a couple and only to mark the ones that correspond with what you want to focus on fixing — Tow Truck connections, Magic c formations, letter size variation, etc.

Give the Check Your Teaching: You can give this easy handwriting check to your students to see if they learned what you taught them. Use it after teaching each letter group, or give it to a child all at once to see what they already know and what they need.

On a blank sheet of paper, draw a single line and have the child write:

CURSIVE		**PRINTING***	
dad g	checks the letters **a d g**	**cows**	checks the letters **c o s v w**
hat cap	checks **h t p**	**cat dog**	checks the letters **a d g**
elf	checks **e l f**	**I like you.**	checks the letters **l k y j u i e**
jiffy up	checks **u y i j**	**run jump bath**	checks the letters **p r n m h b**
kiss rip	checks **k r s**	**fax quiz**	checks the letters **f q x z**
we be or	checks Tow Truck letters		
on am	checks **m** and **n**		
ox quiz	checks **x q z**		

*For more information on HWT's printing strategies read the *K, 1st, or 2nd Grade Printing Teacher's Guide.*

Keep practice short: Ten or fifteen minutes is long enough. You want the child's full attention and optimum effort during the lesson. Then end the lesson while it's still going well or the minute you've lost the child's interest.

Use imitation: What is imitation? It is watching someone do something first, then doing it yourself. With imitation, the child has the opportunity to see how a letter is written; to see the actual movements that were responsible for making the mark. Then the child can associate the trace with the movement that produced it. This is crucial because we are as concerned with how a letter is formed as with how the end product looks. Imitation has two advantages:
1. It gives the child the best chance to write the letter.
2. It teaches the child to correct motor habits.

We are convinced that imitation has been neglected and should be rediscovered with appreciation.

Communicate: Share helpful secrets with others. If you want to help a child with handwriting, the best thing you can do is to get everyone on the same page. As long as everyone knows what is needed, you can move the remediation along. Use the Handwriting All Year activities on page 120 to send mini homework assignments home for parent and child to share.

Consistency and Follow-Through: Identify the problems, set-up the team, and let the progress begin. If everyone is being consistent, you will see progress in the child's handwriting.

Help Others: You may develop a love for helping children with handwriting. With HWT workshop training and the HWT program, you can be certified in handwriting.

STRATEGIES FOR A PHYSICAL APPROACH

Handedness

By the time formal handwriting training begins, a child should have developed hand dominance. Sometimes you have to help the child choose the more skilled hand and then facilitate use of that hand. Collaborate with parents, teachers, therapists, and other significant individuals in the child's life to determine the more skilled hand. Create a checklist of activities for everyone to observe (brushing teeth, eating, dressing, cutting, etc.) Together, you can position materials on the preferred side, and encourage use of the most skilled hand for handwriting.

Pencil Grip

Demonstration

Always demonstrate the correct hold and finger positions. Use the Cursive Warm-Ups activity on page 54 in this guide and sing the *Picking Up My Pencil* song, Track 9, on the *Rock, Rap, Tap & Learn* CD.

Correct pencil grip in three easy steps

You can help a child develop a correct pencil grip or fix one that is awkward. The trick is that you don't teach grip by itself. Teach grip in three stages, and you will be impressed with how easy it becomes. The technique takes consistency and a little time. (See page 38 for an illustration of correct grips.) Tell children that you are going to show them a new way to hold their pencils, but that they are not yet allowed to use the new grip for their writing.

1. Pick-Up—Have children pick up the pencil and hold it in the air with the fingers and thumb correctly placed. Help them position their fingers if necessary. Tell your students, "Wow, that is a perfect pencil grip. Now make a few circles in the air with the perfect pencil grip. Drop it and do it again." Repeat this five times a day for a couple of weeks.

2. Scribble-wiggle—Give students a piece of paper with five randomly placed dots. Have them pick up the pencil, hold it correctly, and put the pencil point on the dot. The little finger side of the pencil hand rests on the paper. Students make wiggly marks through and around the dot without lifting their pencils or hands. (The helping hand is flat and holds the paper.) The advantage of this step is that children develop their pencil grip and finger control without being critical of how the writing looks. Do this daily for a couple weeks.

3. Write—Have students pick up the pencil, hold it correctly, and write the first letter of their names. Add letters until the children can write their names easily with the correct grip. Once they are writing letters with their new grip, grant them permission to use it for all their writing.

Drive the Pencil Trick

(This is a summary of a tip from Betsy Daniel, COTA/L and Christine Bradshaw, OTR/L.) Name the fingers: The thumb is the dad, and the index finger is the mom. The remaining fingers are the child and any brothers, sisters, friends, or pets. Say the pencil is the car. Just as in a real car, dad and mom sit in front and the kids, friends, or pets sit in back. For safe driving, dad shouldn't sit on mom's lap (thumb on top of index finger), and mom never sits on dad's lap (index finger on top of thumb)! If children use an overlapping or tucked-in thumb, remind them that no one can sit on anyone's lap while driving!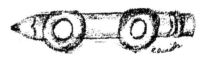

Adaptive Devices

If a child continues to have difficulty holding the pencil, there are a variety of grips available at school supply stores, art/stationary stores, and catalogs. Their usefulness varies from grip-to-grip and child-to-child. Experiment with them, and use them only if they make it easier for the child to hold the pencil correctly. With young children, physical devices should not be used as substitutes for physical demonstration.

Rubber Band Trick: Check the angle of the pencil. If it's standing straight up, the pencil will be hard to hold and will cause tension in the fingertips. Put a rubber band around the child's wrist. Loop another rubber band to the first one. Pull the loop over the pencil eraser. This may keep the pencil pulled back at the correct angle. You may make or buy a more comfortable version that uses ponytail holders.

Reward a Grip

Sometimes young children need motivation to use their new grip. You can offer them a small reward for remembering how to hold their pencils correctly. Track their progress so they can see how close they are to reaching their reward. Attach a photo of their correct pencil grip with a small strip of paper to their desks and stamp them every time you catch them holding their pencil correctly. Thus you help them build a good motor pattern.

Check My Grip	Look at me, I'm holding my pencil correctly.

① ② ③ ④ ⑤   My reward is:

⑥ ⑦ ⑧ ⑨ ⑩

Pencil Pressure

Sometimes children have to learn to judge and moderate their pencil pressure. It's more common for a child to push too hard than not hard enough. Regardless, both can cause problems.

Too hard: Try a mechanical pencil so the child has to control the amount of pressure. You can also have children place the paper on a mouse pad (if they press too hard they will poke holes in their paper).*

Too soft: Have the child pencil in small shapes until they are black. Use pencils with softer lead.

*Suggestions should be tried at home before they're used at school, because remedies for pencil pressure problems can be frustrating to the child.

Posture

Children will sacrifice all stability for mobility. They love to move! Children need to sit in their chairs with their hips, knees, and feet at a 90-degree angle. Check the furniture size. The chair and desk should fit the child. If you can't find a smaller chair, place something (a phone book, box, etc.) under the child's feet for stability. This will help them to sit up when it's time to write.

Helper Hand

Where is the helping hand; the hand that isn't holding the pencil? We've all seen helping hands in laps, twirling hair, or propping up foreheads. You can nag the child, but you'll get better results if you talk directly to the hand! Try it! Take the child's helping hand in yours and pretend to talk to that hand.

Name the helping hand. For example: Ask John what other name he likes that starts with **J**. If John says "Jeremy," tell him that you are going to name his helping hand "Jeremy." Have a little talk with Jeremy, the helping hand. Tell Jeremy that he's supposed to help by holding the paper. Say that John is working really hard on his handwriting, but he needs Jeremy's help. Show Jeremy where he's supposed to be. Tell John that he might have to remind Jeremy about his job.

Kids think this is a hoot. They don't get embarrassed because it's the helping hand, not them, that is being corrected. It's not John who needs to improve, it's Jeremy. This is a face-saving, but effective, reminder. Flat fingers please! A flat (but not stiff) helping hand promotes relaxed writing. Put your hand flat on the table and try to feel tension—there isn't any! Make a fist and feel the tension! Children can get uptight while writing, but a flat helping hand decreases tension.

STRATEGIES FOR SELF-CORRECTION

Sometimes children are fine with handwriting, but they over- or under-correct their work. You can download tools to remediate these issues at **www.hwtears.com/click**.

The Eraser Challenge

Some children spend a lot of time erasing. Those who erase often tend to be slow and lag behind in their work. If you want to control the amount of erasing without taking away erasers, strike a deal using the following strategy:

1. Download the Eraser Flags.
2. Tape them to your students' desks or send them home for parents to use when helping with homework.
3. Every time children erase, they pull a flag.
4. Play a game by challenging children to have a certain amount of flags left at the end of the day.

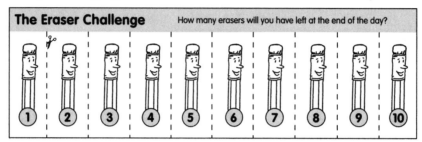

The Eraser Challenge   How many erasers will you have left at the end of the day?

① ② ③ ④ ⑤ ⑥ ⑦ ⑧ ⑨ ⑩

Spot Good Writing

Some children have good handwriting skills but don't carry them over into general school work. Make your expectations clear and make children accountable. Download and print these notes to help children improve what's good and what's not.

SPOT GOOD WRITING
Can you check all of these?
☐ Strokes - start, sequence of letters good
☐ Sit letters on line
☐ Size of letters seems suitable
☐ Spaces in sentences
☐ Start with a CAPITAL
☐ Stop with a ? !
☐ See if others can read
© 2008 Handwriting Without Tears®

Spacing

For printing remediation, teach your students to put letters in a word close to each other. Have them put their index fingers up and bring them close together, without touching. Tell them, "In a word, the letters are close, but don't touch." Draw fingers for them.

Sentence Spacing with Pennies

Give your children pennies or chips to use. Teach them how to look at a short simple sentence and fix the pennies to match as in this example.

I   see   a   dog.

Sick Sentence Clinic

The teacher writes a sentence with the words too close. Children underline each word in the sentence. Now copy the sentence over with spaces between the words.

Icanrun.   I   can   run.

The Nothing Bottle

If students run their words together:

Say that you will give them what they need for spaces. Have them hold out their hands to catch it. Take a huge empty bottle (or any container) and make a big show of pouring into their hands. Ask, "What did you get?" Nothing! tell them to put nothing after every word they write.

Nothing Bottle

STRATEGIES FOR PRINTING & CURSIVE SKILLS

Memory

Bolded activities represents activities found in our K, 1st, or 2nd Grade Printing Teacher's Guides.

- Play visual memory games with capital and lowercase flashcards.
- **Use HWT readiness materials (Wood Pieces Set, Capital Letter Cards, Stamp and See Screen).**
- Go on letter scavenger hunts. Look for things around the school or house that begin with letters that need to be practiced.
- Build a letter card repertoire. Start with just the letters that the child can name instantly. Add one new letter at a time.

Orientation

- Correct number reversals by choosing one reversal per assignment. If children reverse many of their numbers, work on them one at a time beginning with the lowest number. Master that formation before moving on to another number.
- Use Wet–Dry–Try. **The Slate Chalkboard works for capitals and number reversals**. Use the Blackboard with Double Lines for lowercase letters.
- **Play the Mystery Letter game using Gray Blocks or Slate.**

Placement

- Teach bumping the lines using the Blackboard with Double Lines and Wet–Dry–Try.
- Under Over activity, page 25 of this guide.
- Do demonstration/imitation of small, tall, descending letter placement.
- **Do Letter Size and Place activities (2nd Grade Printing Teacher's Guide) followed by writing letters or words on double lines.**
- Model how different paper is used and how letters sit on the lines.

Size

- Use paper that promotes an age–appropriate letter size.
- Avoid poorly designed worksheets: overly busy, confusing lines, inadequate room for writing.
- Use landscape rather than portrait worksheets.

Start/Sequence

- Demonstrate/imitate to build correct habits for letters.
- **For printing- Teach the TOP!**
- **Use ☺ cue to help children notice the top left corner.**
- **Use Slate Chalkboard with Wet–Dry–Try.**
- **Use Gray Block Paper.**

Spacing

- Teach spacing actively.
- Use worksheets that model generous spacing: horizontal, landscape format if possible.
- **Use the Sentence Song on the Rock, Rap, Tap & Learn CD, Track 7.**
- Use Sentence Spacing with Pennies, page 118 of this guide.
- Teach children about spacing using their fingers, page 118 of this guide.
- Teach the Sick Sentence Clinic, page 118 of this guide.
- Use the Nothing Bottle activity, page 118 of this guide.

Control

- Correct children's other printing/cursive skills to help improve their control.
- Consult an occupational therapist if you suspect that control is affected by a fine motor problem (clue: all other skills are okay, but control is poor).

Connections

- Demonstration is important, so demonstrate connections or your students.
- Use Wet–Dry–Try. The Blackboard with Double Lines is a great way to practice connections. See page 24.
- Use Review and Mastery games
- When working with a group of children, use the Connection Inspection activity.

STRATEGIES FOR OTHER METHODS AND HOME PRACTICE
Other Methods
Children in your classroom may have learned other styles of handwriting. Support and accept those other styles, but only if they work. If a particular style is giving a child problems with speed or neatness, you will have to decide whether to modify or reteach it.

Typically, elaborate slanted cursive is something that can be modified. For example, you can teach children to eliminate unnecessary tails and start strokes that may be causing problems. You can even take away the slant.

If the style is delaying the child's academics, then it might be best to re-teach. For example, cursive capitals can be very simple to write. Consider taking away the slant and any unnecessary tails.

Handwriting All Year
What do you do when the workbook is complete? You continue with short lessons to maintain and improve cursive skills. You might like to follow a weekly routine. We have ideas for every day of the week. Here are just a few:

Monday: Capital Letters
Capitals in the News
Create lists of current events to practice capitals. Select people and places that are in the news from the front page of the newspaper.

Tuesday: Lowercase Letters and Connections
Tricky Connections
In this weeks spelling tests, pull out words that use o w b and v.

Wednesday: Words
Verbs-Present and Past Tense
- Have students write the past tense of verbs. For example: bake/baked, call/called, float/floated, hug/hugged, listen/listened, move/moved, nap/napped, plan/planned, rip/ripped, save/saved.

Thursday: Sentence Skills and Punctuation
Similes and Metaphors in Sentences
Similes are figures of speech that compare things. They make sentences come alive! Similes use the words "like" or "as" to make comparisons. For example: Kirstin swims like a fish.
- Write a sentence that uses a simile - like a fish, as a mouse, as a statue, like a snail, as a turtle. Metaphors are also figures of speech that compare things but metaphors do not use "like" or "as." For example: Eric is a bundle of energy.

Friday: Free Choice
Independent writing
Children can write a paragraph in cursive about a topic of their choice.

EXTRAS

We include here a few final things that are essential to facilitating good handwriting instruction.

Report Card Insert

Some report cards don't have a place to grade or mark handwriting success. This is particularly important in the younger grades because handwriting performance can affect other academic subjects. If your report card doesn't allow space for handwriting, use this downloadable form and include it with your students' report cards. It will send the message that you value handwriting and are monitoring handwriting progress.

Handwriting Report Name					
Cursive Skill	**Q1**	**Q2**	**Q3**	**Q4**	**Comments**
Forms capitals correctly					
Forms lowercase correctly					
Correct connections					
Writes on lines					
Writes appropriate size					
Apples skills					

Educating Others

Because handwriting often takes a backseat in today's elementary schools, it's wonderful for someone knowledgeable in handwriting, specifically the Handwriting Without Tears® method, to step forward and share that knowledge with others. Whether you are educating parents at a back-to-school night or presenting in front of a language arts committee, the information you share will improve the likelihood that others will recognize the importance of teaching handwriting.

Parents

Educate parents about HWT, pencil grip, and cursive skills. Giving parents letter charts at the start of school helps them to understand how to form letters and help their children at home. You can find parent articles at **www.hwtears.com/click** that you can print and distribute.

Colleagues

Share your HWT knowledge with your friends and co-workers. If you have attended or plan to attend our workshops, tell friends about it, or—better yet—invite them to come along. Often, all it takes is one teacher from a school getting excited about handwriting and HWT to get an entire school interested in learning more.

Administrators and Committees

Principals can be your biggest advocates. Share the information you have learned with principals and other administrators. Discuss the benefits of handwriting consistency and how HWT can help. Many HWT advocates have successfully written proposals, initiated handwriting pilot studies, presented to language arts committees, and seen large districts adopt HWT district wide. Email or call us for help - janolsen@hwtears.com or 301-263-2700. We will send you a CD loaded with everything you need to help others understand that handwriting should be an easy victory for children and how using Handwriting Without Tears® enables that success.

Teaching Guidelines

The HWT curriculum is highly adaptable and can be used in a number of ways. If you are looking for a completely structured approach, we created these guidelines to help you along.

Week	Monday	Tuesday	Wednesday	Thursday	Friday
1	**Cursive Warm-Up Under and over** TG3rd pg. 55 CH pg. 7	**Cursive Warm-Up Under and over** TG3rd pg. 55 CH pg. 7	**Cursive Warm-Up Up and straight down** TG3rd pg. 55 CH pg. 7	**Cursive Warm-Up Up and straight down** TG3rd pg. 55 CH pg. 7	**Cursive Warm-Up Up and loop down** TG3rd pg. 55 CH pg. 7
2	**Cursive Warm-up Up and Loop Down** TG3rd pg. 55 CH pg. 7	**Cursive Warm-Up Descending loop** TG3rd pg. 55 CH pg. 7	**Cursive Warm-Up Descending loop** TG3rd pg. 55 CH pg. 7	*cc* TG3rd pg. 57 CH pg. 8-9	*cc* TG3rd pg. 57 CH pg. 8-9
3	*a* TG3rd pg. 58 CH pg. 10-11	**Connections** TG3rd pg. 58 CH pg. 11	*d* TG3rd pg. 59 CH pg. 12-13	**Connections** TG3rd pg. 59 CH pg. 13	**Word Practice** TG3rd pg. 59 CH pg. 12-13
4	*g* TG3rd pg. 60 CH pg. 14-15	**Connections** TG3rd pg. 60 CH pg. 15	**Word Practice** TG3rd pg. 60 CH pg. 14-15	*cc* **Mystery Letter Game** TG3rd pg. 61	*cc* **Mystery Letter Game** TG3rd pg. 61
5	*h* TG3rd pg. 62 CH pg. 16-17	**Connections** TG3rd pg. 62 CH pg. 16-17	*t* TG3rd pg. 63 CH pg. 18-19	**Connections** TG3rd pg. 63 CH pg. 18-19	**Word Practice** TG3rd pg. 62-63 CH pg. 18-19
6	*p* TG3rd pg. 64 CH pg. 20-21	**Connections** TG3rd pg. 64 CH pg. 20-21	*l* TG3rd pg. 65 CH pg. 22-23	**Connections** TG3rd pg. 65 CH pg. 22-23	**Word Practice** TG3rd pg. 64-65 CH pg. 22-23
7	*l* TG3rd pg. 66 CH pg. 24-25	**Word Practice** TG3rd pg. 66 CH pg. 24-25	*f* TG3rd pg. 67 CH pg. 26-27	**Word Practice** TG3rd pg. 67 CH pg. 26-27	**Review & Mastery Cursive to Cursive** TG3rd pg. 68 CH pg. 28
8	**Review & Mastery Cursive to Cursive** TG3rd pg. 68 CH pg. 29	**Review & Mastery Print to Cursive** TG3rd pg. 69 CH pg. 30	**Review & Mastery Silly Spelling** TG3rd pg. 69 CH pg. 31	*u* TG3rd pg. 70 CH pg. 32-33	**Word Practice** TG3rd pg. 70 CH pg. 32-33
9	*y* TG3rd pg. 71 CH pg. 34-35	**Word Practice** TG3rd pg. 71 CH pg. 34-35	*i* TG3rd pg. 72 CH pg. 36-37	**Word Practice** TG3rd pg. 72 CH pg. 36-37	*j* TG3rd pg. 73 CH pg. 38-39

Week	Monday	Tuesday	Wednesday	Thursday	Friday
10	**Word Practice** TG3rd pg. 73 CH pg. 38-39	**Review & Mastery Cursive to Cursive** TG3rd pg. 74 CH pg. 40	**Review & Mastery Silly Spelling** TG3rd pg. 75 CH pg. 41	*k* TG3rd pg. 76 CH pg. 42-43	**Word Practice** TG3rd pg. 76 CH pg. 42-43
11	*M* TG3rd pg. 77 CH pg. 44-45	**Word Practice** TG3rd pg. 77 CH pg. 44-45	*A* TG3rd pg. 78 CH pg. 46-47	**Word Practice** TG3rd pg. 78 CH pg. 46-47	**Review & Mastery Cursive to Cursive** TG3rd pg. 79 CH pg. 48
12	**Review & Mastery Silly Spelling** TG3rd pg. 80 CH pg. 49	*O* TG3rd pg. 82 CH pg. 50-51	**Word Practice** TG3rd pg. 82 CH pg. 50-51	*W* TG3rd pg. 83 CH pg. 52-53	**Word Practice** TG3rd pg. 83 CH pg. 52-53
13	*b* TG3rd pg. 84 CH pg. 54-55	**Word Practice** TG3rd pg. 84 CH pg. 54-55	*V* TG3rd pg. 85 CH pg. 56-57	**Word Practice** TG3rd pg. 85 CH pg. 56-57	**Crank Up Letters** TG3rd pg. 86 CH pg. 58-59
14	**Crank Up Letters** TG3rd pg. 87 CH pg. 60-61	**Review & Mastery Cursive to Cursive** TG3rd pg. 88 CH pg. 62	**Review & Mastery Silly Spelling** TG3rd pg. 89 CH pg. 63	*m* TG3rd pg. 90 CH pg. 64-65	**Word Practice** TG3rd pg. 90 CH pg. 64-65
15	*m* TG3rd pg. 91 CH pg. 66-67	**Word Practice** TG3rd pg. 91 CH pg. 66-67	**Tow Truck Letters** TG3rd pg. 92 CH pg. 68-69	**Review & Mastery** TG3rd pg. 93-94 CH pg. 70-71	*X* TG3rd pg. 95 CH 72-73
16	*q* TG3rd pg. 96 CH pg. 74-75	**Word Practice** TG3rd pg. 95-96 CH pg. 74-75	*z* TG3rd pg. 97 CH pg. 76-77	**Word Practice** TG3rd pg. 97 CH pg. 76-77	**Review & Mastery** TG3rd pg. 98-99 CH pg. 78-79
17	*CaOU* TG3rd pg. 101 CH pg. 80	*VWXYz* TG3rd pg. 102 CH pg. 81	*PBRNMH* TG3rd pg. 103 CH pg. 82	*KJILID* TG3rd pg. 104 CH pg. 83	*LDSE2* TG3rd pg. 105 CH pg. 84
18	***Review Lowercase and Connections**	***Review Capital Letters**	***Word Practice**	***Sentence Pages**	***Activity Pages** TG3rd pg.106-112

* Make Reviewing Letters fun by using multisensory lessons.   ***3rd Grade Cursive Teacher's Guide***

FAQs

Why aren't there any grade levels on your workbooks?
In some instances, we recommend that an older child be taught using a workbook from a lower grade. We don't want the child to feel bad, so we remove the grade level. Thus we focus on the skill, not the grade level.

Why do you teach cursive capital 𝒜 the way you do?
𝒜 begins on the bottom line with a curved stroke up, like writing **C** from the bottom. It's an easier letter for children when it starts on the baseline like 𝒥. If children want to start it from the left to be able to connect it and can do so without difficulty, it's fine to teach it that way.

Why do you teach the c to a connections first? Wouldn't a baseline to baseline connection be easier to teach?
c and **a** are frequently used letters that are similar in formation to their printed counterparts. The **c** to **a** connection is the foundation skill for cursive connections. Mastering **c** to **a** established good habits for the rest of the cursive connections.

Why don't all of the capital letters connect to the next lowercase letter when you write a cursive word or proper noun that starts with a capital?
HWT teaches children to connect lowercase letters to a capital when the capital letter ends on the baseline and on the right side of the capital letter (the side closest to the lowercase letter they want to connect). HWT teaches this skill to children to make the process of learning and writing capital letters easier. There are 4 different types of connections that can occur between letters and they are dependent on the 2 letters to be joined together. The frequency of capital letter usage is low compared to lowercase in writing. Instructional time for connection skills is more effectively spent on lowercase letters.

Why do you have the students practice the under curve/over curve activity with their left hand?
It's a large movement that takes the child from left to right across their body like they do when writing on a page; they work from left to right. This gross motor skill will translate to fine motor movements regardless of their hand dominance, left or right.

Why do you allow for a printed Q instead of a cursive one?
We recognize that the cursive capital Q is difficult and can be confused with number 2. It's a personal choice, a style preference that will not affect students' ability to read cursive or affect their legibility in written cursive.

Is cursive faster than print?
Yes! When we connect letters together, our writing speed increases. When children are first learning cursive, cursive can be slower than print. When they begin the mastery stage, you will notice speed gradually increasing. Mastering connection skills and making cursive a part of your students' everyday school work will enable them to build natural and automatic skills for cursive that will improve their writing speed.

Why do so many kids stop doing cursive?
There is a lack of follow-through and practice in the school day when instruction has been completed. Children must be required to use these newly learned skills so that they may fully master and develop natural and automatic skills in cursive. Cursive has to be a priority in the 3rd, 4th, and 5th grades for children to fully develop cursive skill. Most children are taught cursive but are never required to use it.

Which letter is the boss of the connection? The first or the second?
The first letter is always the boss of the connection and will determine where the connection will begin and how the next letter is connected. The second letter does affect the connection, but it is the first letter that always begins the connection. Therefore, it is the boss. See page 10 of this guide.

Lowercase Letter Frequency Chart

The 220 words on the Dolch List were published by Dr. Edward Dolch in 1948. The words are the most frequently found words in books that children in Grades K–3 read. Naturally, these are also the words that children frequently write. By counting how many times each letter appears on the list, we determined individual letter frequency. This chart shows each letter in order of decreasing frequency. With this information, teachers can make priority decisions about correcting and reviewing letters.

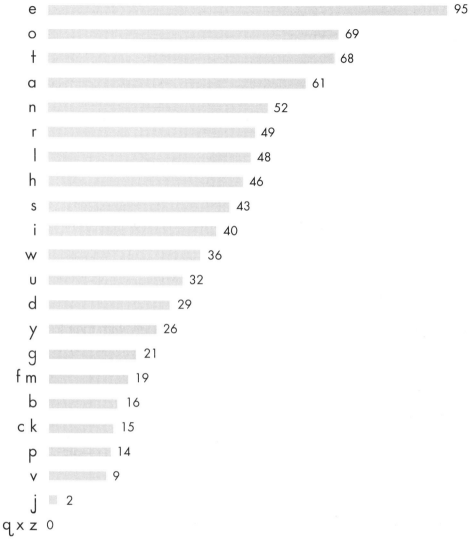

Letter	Frequency
e	95
o	69
t	68
a	61
n	52
r	49
l	48
h	46
s	43
i	40
w	36
u	32
d	29
y	26
g	21
f m	19
b	16
c k	15
p	14
v	9
j	2
q x z	0

The Top 40 Words

Mastering frequently used words is important for cursive fluency. Use this list from the Dolch sight words for practice and review. Be sure to avoid words that use letters you haven't taught yet.

1. the	11. his	21. with	31. be
2. to	12. that	22. up	32. have
3. and	13. she	23. all	33. go
4. he	14. for	24. look	34. we
5. you	15. on	25. is	35. am
6. it	16. they	26. her	36. then
7. of	17. but	27. there	37. little
8. in	18. had	28. some	38. down
9. was	19. at	29. out	39. do
10. said	20. him	30. as	40. can

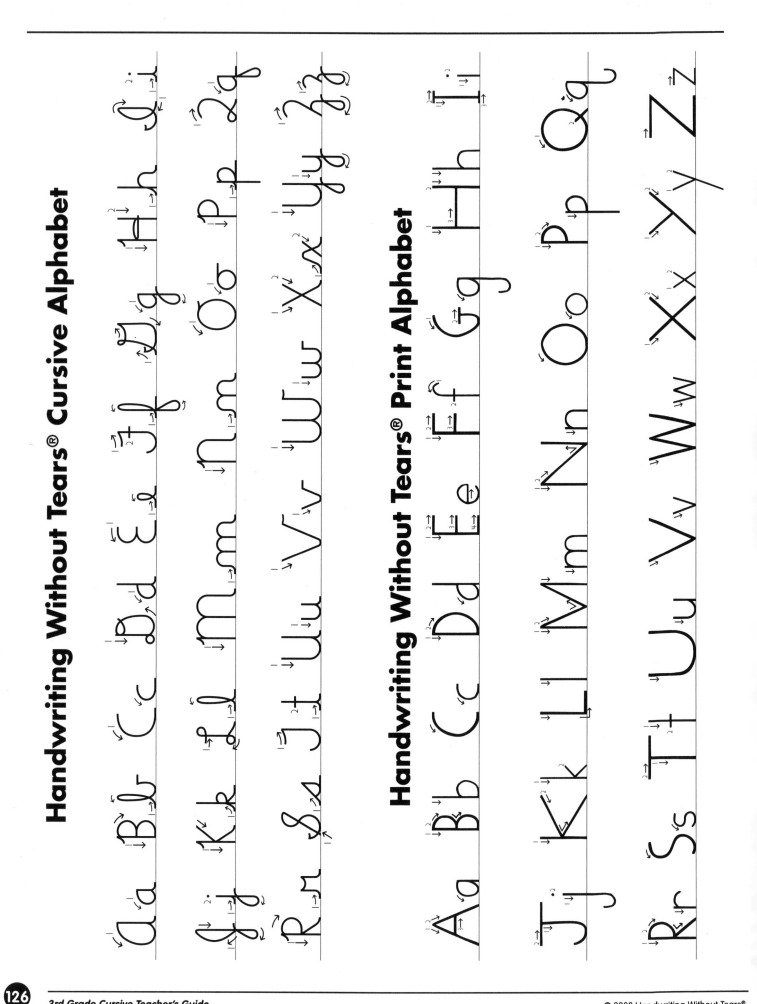

Handwriting Without Tears® Cursive Alphabet

Handwriting Without Tears® Print Alphabet